Hongiou Fortune

Wealth for Generations

Honglou Fortune

Wealth for Generations

汇丰  晋信

HSBC Jintrust Fund Management

Translated by

Khaw Weikang

WILEY

John Wiley & Sons, Inc.

Other Wiley Editorial Offices

John Wiley & Sons, 111 River Street, Hoboken, NJ 07030, USA

John Wiley & Sons, The Atrium, Southern Gate, Chichester, West Sussex, P019 8SQ, United Kingdom

John Wiley & Sons (Canada) Ltd., 5353 Dundas Street West, Suite 400, Toronto, Ontario, M9B 6HB, Canada

John Wiley & Sons Australia Ltd, 42 McDougall Street, Milton, Queensland 4064, Australia

Wiley-VCH, Boschstrasse 12, D-69469 Weinheim, Germany

Library of Congress Cataloging-in-Publication Data

ISBN 978-0-470-82434-4

Typeset in 11.5/14pt Bembo by Aptara Inc., New Delhi, India.
Printed in Singapore by Saik Wah Press Pte. Ltd.

10 9 8 7 6 5 4 3 2 1

Contents

Foreword

The world's attention is currently focused on China. But what is the focus of the Chinese? The answer is wealth management. Wealth management has become an everyday topic, immediately following basic survival. An often-heard sentiment that epitomizes the wealth management attitude of the average Chinese today is: "You can fall behind Liu Xiang (Olympic men's 110m hurdles gold medalist), but you definitely can't fall behind the consumer price index!" Having gone through the financial crisis, many of the average investors in China have finally discovered the vast difference between managing and not managing their wealth!

However, China does not have a very long history in the financial markets, with its stock market having only just reached "maturity" (18 years). Trusts, funds, pensions—the mainland Chinese are only beginning to get acquainted with investment tools that have been popular overseas for many years. Therefore, it is a general phenomenon that everyone talks about wealth management, but few actually know how to achieve it. The majority of people either keep their money in the banks or buy treasury bonds. In 2007, China's population's savings deposits totaled a whopping RMB1.7 trillion (US$242.8 billion)! In the same year, the penetration of Chinese bank accounts investing in funds was only 3–4 percent, with penetration in families at 3 percent, a far cry from 33 percent and 51 percent respectively, in the United States.

Why have the investment modes of the Chinese people remained so conservative? This is largely attributed to the general consensus of average people that investing is too complicated. Financial assets are intangible, unlike consumer goods that can be seen and touched, so they are difficult for investors to comprehend. Investors either become very apprehensive when making decisions, resulting in less than optimal timing, or they do not have a clear understanding of the basic concepts throughout the entire investment process and end up making erroneous judgments by choosing the wrong investment products or exiting the market too early.

If learning about investments were simplified, people could become more financially astute. With precisely this objective in mind, investment specialist HSBC Jintrust has embarked on its educational endeavor. Armed with a better understanding of investment concepts, funds and various investment products, people would realize that investing can be a very straightforward and lighthearted affair.

So how can learning about investments occur almost subconsciously while readers experience the joys of reading? This is where *Honglou Meng* or *Dream of the Red Chamber* comes into play. It is one of China's four great classical novels that almost every Chinese national has heard. There is no lack of mention of investment and wealth management in the book, either. "Who among the thousands of men could manage the country, yet just a lady or two to set the household right?" Under the pen of author Cao Xue Qin, the "leading figures among the ladies" have all become worthy exponents of wealth management. Doesn't Wang Xi Feng already know how to "grow dollars from pennies"?

Therefore, we send Tan Chun to Harvard to become a wealth management expert; Wang Xi Feng fails in her investments in bonds and securities, causing the splitting of finances in the Jia household; Li Wan is pleased with her son Jia Lan when he displays a good "financial quotient"; Bao Yu's funds are tied up in stocks and he sacrifices for Dai Yu's poetry series. Inheriting the original characters and their personalities from *Honglou Meng* to develop a novel storyline with a twist, the unchanging principles of wealth management and investment are depicted through the overlapping of ancient and modern times.

Upon completing this book, each reader will be one step closer to realizing his or her dreams of true financial freedom.

Steve Lee
CEO
HSBC Jintrust Fund Management

Chapter 1

The Matriarch
Cautions the
Youngsters

An "Idol" Competition is Launched

One day, the poetry club of the Grand Garden met to discuss the differences between Western and Eastern mysticism shown in the film *Wu Ji*. The members—Bao Yu, Bao Chai, Dai Yu, Xiang Yun, Ying Chun, Tan Chun, and Xi Chun—all gathered at Li Wan's Fragrant Paddy Fields, which the eldest daughter-in-law was in charge of. Xiang Yun re-enacted a scene where Princess Qingcheng stood on the city wall and spoke to the soldiers, which made everyone laugh. At the height of their excitement, a servant came in to report the arrival of Matriarch Jia.

Everyone stood up hastily as Xi Feng, the second eldest daughter-in-law, helped the frail matriarch into the room. Upon entering, Sister Feng winked repeatedly at Li Wan, but the eldest daughter-in-law failed to grasp her hint. This prompted Sister Feng to point at Grandmother Jia discreetly, and then wave her hand as though to caution Li Wan about what she should say.

Li Wan observed Grandmother Jia intently, and noticed her eyes were red and puffy and her expression mournful. Surprised yet curious, she asked, "How are you, Mother-in-law?"

Grandmother Jia sighed and said, "All you youngsters know is how to have fun in the Grand Garden. Do you realize that we are being criticized by others?" Silence filled the room, and after a pause, she continued, "There is a person named Leng Zi Xing (literally meaning 'wet blanket') who spoke about the younger generation of eminent and well-off families like us going from bad to worse. Both masters and servants live lavish lifestyles, yet none know about wealth planning. He even claimed our wealth would not last beyond three generations!"

Li Wan pulled Sister Feng aside and asked softly, "Why is Grandmother Jia angry out of the blue?"

Sister Feng responded, "The Zheng Family from Jiang Nan came over today to inform us that their matriarch had passed away. They told us that seconds before the old lady drew her last breath, she lamented, 'I've been thrifty all my life, yet the wealth that I painstakingly accumulated is now for others to enjoy.' Grandmother Jia was not pleased when she heard the news. She flew into a rage when she heard the impudent remarks made by others."

While Li Wan and Sister Feng were talking, Grandmother Jia let out another long sigh and said, "All along, I never intended to interfere in your affairs, but now I worry that our family's wealth will be squandered even before I've passed away. I'm not afraid of poverty, but how can I live in peace if that actually happens?"

Upon hearing these remarks, everyone consoled the matriarch. Grandmother Jia, now calmer, continued, "From now on, you all need to change your mindsets. There's an old saying, 'If a person fails to plan, he plans to fail.' Even though you are all still young, wealth management should not be treated lightly. If you fail to make financial plans, how will you support yourself in your old age? There's another popular saying, 'If you ignore wealth management, wealth will ignore you.' All of you are intelligent; you should understand my point. Besides having a humanities club, history club, and literature club, it is also vital to have a wealth management club." Everyone nodded in agreement.

Sister Feng laughed. "Grandmother's words have enlightened all of us. I am sure learning wealth management will be beneficial to the youngsters, but where do they start?"

Grandmother Jia paused, and said thoughtfully, "That's a good point. In that case, I'll pose a question. Whoever gets the correct answer, I'll use my own savings to send him or her overseas to study. After that, he or she can impart the knowledge to the others."

Sister Feng laughed again. "Mother-in-law, you are really such a big fan of the Idol competition that you want to hold a competition within our household?"

Grandmother Jia laughed with her. "It's called keeping pace with the times!"

What question did the matriarch pose? Read on to find out.

HSBC Jintrust investment advisors recommend:

The most important move in wealth management is taking the first step

The greatest obstacle to wealth management is neither choosing a style nor a method; rather it is one's mentality. If a person knows only how to work for money and not how money can work for him or her, this person will not be able to escape from the traditional, conservative "Grand Garden" of the mind.

Chapter 2

The Matriarch of the Grand Garden Poses a Question

The Girls Talk Wealth Management in a Bid for Selection

Grandmother Jia decided to pose a question to assess the girls' financial acumen. She began, "I'm going to pose a cliché question. Nonetheless, I want an intelligent and novel answer."

Before she could pose the question, Bao Yu interrupted. "Grandmother, I would like an opportunity to further my studies, too."

Xiang Yun laughed. "Don't worry, you're one of us. We won't leave you out." Everyone laughed together and Grandmother Jia asked, "Why do we need wealth management?"

Bao Yu clapped his hands and replied confidently, "Grand-mother, you posed such a simple question. Let me try to answer!" He assumed a scholarly air, bobbing his head up and down, and began speaking. "The phrase 'wealth management' literally means to manage one's assets, to further one's wealth. However, that should be left to the men. Girls should not meddle in such is-sues. Their ignorance will only be a hindrance. Any windfall will become a downfall; any fortune will become a misfortune."

A normally restrained Dai Yu decided to speak her mind: "If you are in a well, you can only see a small piece of the sky; when you are held down by prejudices by the common man, how can you ever rise above them?" The matriarch heard this but did not utter a word.

Bao Chai added, "Bao Yu, you call yourself our best friend, so why discriminate against our gender? Guys may be more know-ledgable than we are about wealth management, but in terms of hands-on application, girls are on par with the guys. Take, for instance, Sister Feng. She did a great job of taking care of such a big family. No man is comparable. Then look at Tan Chun. She contracted out the maintenance work in the gardens. This saves us $400 to $500 a year. She is arguably the pioneer of outsourcing."

Bao Yu immediately replied, "That's true. I was wrong about wealth management."

Tan Chun laughed. "Grandmother Jia is testing our knowledge of wealth management. Why did you end up talking about me? In my opinion, it is vital that everyone engage in wealth man-agement. Take, for instance, the rising inflation our country is experiencing! Should one not bother about wealth management, with an annual inflation rate of 5 percent, what is $1,000,000 to-day will only be worth $600,000 in 10 years—$400,000 will have been lost."

When Grandmother Jia heard this, she recalled asking her ser-vant Yuan Yang to open her safe and count her assets. To her dismay, after 10 years of saving, there was not even enough for Bao Yu and Dai Yu's weddings.

Xi Chun, who was standing in a corner, spoke: "Wealth is but an external thing. So what if one person is wealthier than another?"

Ying Chun added, "A lady does not control her destiny. Her wealth depends on her fate."

Tan Chun shook her head in disagreement. "Second Sister, you are too good-natured and dependent, and so you are easily swayed by others' opinions. But for me, I don't want to be at anyone's beck and call. Hence, I must be financially independent."

Xiang Yun pouted. "But even if we do want to practice financial planning, how are we to do so with just $200 per month?"

Tan Chun explained: "Financial planning starts with whatever little wealth one has. Wealthy individuals do not become rich overnight but do so through proper planning so that they increase and multiply their monetary assets. Take, for example, our monthly allowance. Everyone else complains it is insufficient, but with proper planning, I am able to save a sum of money and I have asked Second Brother to help me buy some trinkets." She turned around and took something from the servant behind. It was a scent box woven of bamboo shoots. Xiang Yun and the rest had seldom seen such an object, and they marveled at the box.

Read on to find out Grandmother's comments for the ladies.

HSBC Jintrust investment advisors recommend:

Wealth management protects and adds value to your assets

Why is it vital to understand wealth management? Firstly, it helps maintain the value of your wealth. Secondly, your assets can appreciate in value with proper planning. This will help you to realize your aspirations.

Chapter 3

The Wise Matriarch Explains Inflation

*The Intelligent Tan Chun Fulfills a
Long-Held Wish*

Grandmother Jia paused before speaking again. "I understood all your suggestions, and of them all, I think Tan
Chun's explanation is the best."

Sister Feng laughed. "Mother-in-law, what you've said is right.
Tan Chun is knowledgable and eloquent. She will be a great help
to the household!" Everyone nodded in agreement, except Dai
Yu. She regretted not displaying her talents fully and missing a
great opportunity.

Grandmother Jia continued: "In my opinion, there are two
objectives of wealth management. The first is to suppress the effects
of inflation; the second is to accumulate wealth through investment,
as opposed to scrimping with the already miserly $200 you all
receive every month. Though it is important to save diligently and

be thrifty, being overly stingy does not reflect well on the reputation of our family."

Sister Feng said, "I wonder what the terms inflation, CPI, and negative interest rate that have appeared in recent news mean."

Grandmother Jia laughed. "Many people praise you for your vast experience; even men pale in comparison. Yet you do not know what the news is about!"

Sister Feng protested: "Mother-in-law, your experience and exposure are much wider and richer than mine! Would you teach me?"

Grandmother Jia responded: "CPI is the acronym for Consumer Price Index. The state statistical bureau tracks the prices of a hundred commodities and services and uses these data to formulate the CPI. It also indicates the general trend of commodities. For example, in 2004, the CPI rose by 3.9 percent. This indicates that our living expenses, when compared to the previous year, have risen by 3.9 percent. If the interest rate for bank deposits is 2.25 percent per annum, after deducting an interest tax rate of 20 percent, the actual deposit interest rate is 1.80 percent. Based on the existing CPI of 3.90 percent, the real interest rate is 1.80 percent minus 3.90 percent which gives −2.10 percent. Hence, we would have had a negative interest rate. During this period, should a person invest $10,000 in the bank, wishfully thinking his savings are ensured, he would probably not expect that the value of his savings would only be $9,790 after a year."

Li Wan laughed. "Grandmother Jia, you have explained it fully. Not only is Sister Feng unaware of these terms, but I am also ignorant."

Grandmother Jia continued: "There are more things you do not know. The CPI doesn't fully reflect the actual inflation rate. With property doubling in value every two years, if you do not buy the property now, doesn't it mean you lose the chance to double your wealth? The prices of properties are not included in the data for CPI statistics; only rentals are taken into account. This is one of the reasons people feel that the inflation rate is much higher than the increase reflected in the CPI statistics."

Everyone was impressed with Grandmother Jia's knowledge of wealth management. Sister Feng thought to herself, "Grandmother Jia is so well informed about household matters. I think she already knows I am lending people money. What should I do?" Unknown to everyone, after Grandmother Jia had found out from her servant Yuan Yang that her assets accumulated over many years had devaluated significantly, she asked her servants to find information regarding wealth management on the Internet. This is why she was able to share her wealth management knowledge at length.

Grandmother Jia stood up and spoke: "I'm tired now. Xi Feng, remember later to ask Yuan Yang to take out some of my assets. Help find a good and reputable school and arrange for Tan Chun's admission." After saying that, the Matriarch left with her entourage.

Everyone rushed to congratulate Tan Chun. Bao Chai laughed. "You often grumble that you're unable to carve out a career for yourself like a man could. Now your wish has come true." Tan Chun smiled without saying anything.

Read on to find out what happened next.

HSBC Jintrust investment advisors recommend:

Only investments can stop inflation from eroding your wealth

Due to inflation, your spending power will decrease continually. For instance, at an annual 5 percent inflation rate, $1,000,000 today will become the equivalent of $613,900 in 10 years, which is a loss of 40 percent! In 30 years, you would have only $231,400 left, which means you would have lost almost $800,000, or 77 percent!

An inflation rate of 5 percent might not seem like a big issue at the moment, but a continuous inflation rate of 5 percent annually will affect your assets' values drastically.

It is only through investment that one can overcome inflation. Based on a relatively long historical cycle, stocks and equity funds are effective protection against inflation effects. Between the years 1998 and 2005, China's stock funds (including mixed funds) produced an annual investment profit of 8.49 percent, which is higher than the inflation rate in the same period.

(*Source:* Tianxiang Investment Analysis System)

Chapter 4

Concubine Zhao
Wants to Invest
Impulsively

Li Wan Suggests a Prudent Plan

The news that Matriarch Jia was sending Tan Chun for over-seas study initiated a host of activities. Jia Lian spent days scouting for the best school for Tan Chun, before notifying Grandmother Jia he had found the right one. He informed her: "I've secured a place at Harvard University for her."

Grandmother Jia questioned: "Can this university be compared to Jin Ling University where your father and uncles studied?"

Jia Lian laughed. "It is definitely better." A delighted Grand-mother Jia immediately ordered her servant Yuan Yang to take out her collection of jewelry and give it to Jia Lian to exchange for cash to pay for Tan Chun's school fees and living expenses. Jin Lian promptly did so.

Tan Chun was packing her luggage when Ping-er came happily into her room, placing a heavy bag on the table. Tan Chun asked: "What's inside?" She was astounded when Ping-er untied the bag. Before her eyes were bundles of cash.

Ping-er laughed. "Our second master is careless. He forgot to put the $2 million he got in exchange for the jewelry into the bank. It's up to you to decide what to do with it. Second Mistress is taking care of your travel arrangements, and your visa should be approved in two months." Tan Chun thanked Ping-er profusely.

After escorting Ping-er to the door, Tan Chun stared blankly at the pile of cash, at a loss about what to do. At that instant, a high-spirited Concubine Zhao came into the room, exclaiming, "You have brought honor to our Zhao family." Concubine Zhao was startled when she saw the huge stack of cash on the table. She paused for a moment before speaking. "You don't need all this cash urgently, do you?"

Tan Chun replied: "I'll need it in two months."

Concubine Zhao immediately said, "How about leaving it with me?"

Tan Chun, sensing ill intentions, said, "Mother, come straight to the point."

Concubine Zhao said, "Grandmother Ma-Dao and I are good friends. She just provided me with insider information about a sure-win stock. If we use this money to buy the stock, it might double or triple in two months! Take it as helping me and your brother Huan."

Tan Chun explained: "Stock market speculation is unpredictable and volatile; it can even result in complete losses including the principal sum. After all, I need this money in two months. How can I take such a big risk?"

Concubine Zhao's face darkened and she said, "Now that your wings have matured, you're all ready to forget your roots and fly on to higher ground, eh! Go on, take all the money with you. We'll see how you'll be able to lug such a big load to America!" After saying that, she slammed the door behind her.

Tan Chun was overwhelmed by emotions. Tears flowed down her cheeks, as she wondered how her mother could be so merciless when she knew her daughter would be leaving soon to further her studies.

At that moment, the eldest daughter-in-law Li Wan approached from the direction of Sister Feng's room. She saw a tearful Tan Chun and an angry Concubine Zhao hissing as she walked away. Putting two and two together, Li Wan knew roughly what had happened. She consoled Tan Chun. "You are a rational person. Just put up with her a little longer and things will be all right."

Tan Chun, wiping away her tears, said, "The older she gets, the more muddled she becomes. All she yearns for is petty gains, investing without assessing the risks and knowing whether she can handle them. That's one of the biggest taboos in investments!"

Li Wan then asked: "In your opinion, what kinds of risks can be undertaken?"

Tan Chun explained: "Should an investment go awry, it should not hurt the major financial goals of the individual or family. Only an appropriate amount of risk ought to be undertaken."

Li Wan replied: "Well said! Since you need that amount of cash for your school fees, safeguarding it is definitely top priority." Tan Chun nodded in agreement. Li Wan continued: "I was at the bank today and was introduced to a new product known as a money market fund. Its returns are on par with fixed deposits, yet it offers the flexibility of current deposits. If you decide to sell your funds today, the money from the sale will be deposited into your account the following day. This ensures that you will have access to your money. Instead of depositing the $2 million into the bank, why not buy money market funds?"

Tan Chun chuckled. "Aunt Li Wan, you are right. I heard that money market funds are a cash management tool in other countries. They are the most suitable investments for short-term funds like mine."

Li Wan laughed. "You've yet to go overseas to further your studies, yet you are already singing their praises." Upon hearing that, Tan Chun blushed.

Read on to find out more.

HSBC Jintrust investment advisors recommend:

The amount of risk that one can undertake is closely linked to the investment horizon

The purpose may be similar, but the time span for investments may differ. Take, for instance, saving for a child's education. If the education commences in two months, you will only have an investment time frame of two months. Hence, a low-risk investment plan is recommended. In comparison, if your child is a newborn, you will have a longer investment time frame. You might want to consider higher risk investment plans. Even though some products may be unprofitable in the short term, they will have ample time for profitable returns.

Chapter 5

Tan Chun Ventures into Money Market Funds

Sister Feng Incurs Losses in Warrants Investments

As Li Wan and Tan Chun were discussing money market funds, Tan Chun reached for the calculator, entered some numbers and exclaimed, "What a surprise! Based on last year's money funds' annual growth of 2.3 percent, if I invest $2 million, in two months, I can earn $7,675! It yields $5,700 more than current deposits!"

Li Wan laughed. "With this profit, you'll be able to replenish your wardrobe."

Tan Chun said, "My sisters have given me so much clothing in recent days, I will not be able to finish wearing everything in a year. How about letting me treat everyone to a king crab meal after I have reaped the profits?"

Li Wan clapped in agreement and said, "Good idea! After all, everyone loves to eat crab." They ended their discussion and Li Wan bade Tan Chun goodbye.

The following day, Tan Chun went to the bank and bought money market funds. After two months, the funds had gained thousands of dollars. True to her word, she decided to treat Grandmother Jia and the rest to a meal at a famous crab restaurant called Wang Bao He. The dinner also doubled as a farewell dinner, as Tan Chun's visa had been approved. Everyone arrived together at the restaurant. They were dressed to the nines, as though they were trying to outdo each other. Tan Chun was busy ushering the guests to seats and serving them drinks. After everyone was seated, she washed her hands hurriedly and went to sit beside Grandmother Jia to help her prise the crabs open for crab meat.

Grandmother Jia said to her: "I can help, myself. Go enjoy yourself." Tan Chun urged everyone to eat to his or her heart's content before she returned to her seat and started eating. After having a few drinks, everyone started having conversations and playing games. The atmosphere became lively.

While everybody was having a good time, Sister Feng's servant Ping-er walked into the room, looking flustered. She looked for her mistress and whispered something into her ear. Sister Feng's expression changed immediately. She left her seat promptly, and everyone was bewildered. Curious, Grandmother Jia asked Tan Chun to follow Sister Feng to find out what had happened.

Sister Feng returned home, and found Wang-er standing at the doorway waiting for her. Sister Feng told her servant to leave, while beckoning to Wang-er to enter her room. She asked, "What went wrong?"

Wang-er responded hesitantly: "Last month, the warrants you asked me to buy—they have dropped to less than half their initial value these last two days."

Sister Feng was momentarily stunned by the news. She then enquired further: "Didn't you say your friend was an investment expert in warrants and he had never made a wrong judgment before?"

Wang-er continued: "I went to look for him today, hoping to get an explanation. I never expected his losses were so great that he was on the verge of suicide! Fortunately, I managed to dissuade him from it."

Sister Feng gave an angry snort and said, "Phew. I can't believe he can be called an expert! What did you assure me previously?"

Sister Feng's warrants investments were the result of much deliberation. She realized that using the girls' monthly allowance for illegal money lending was not feasible in the long term. She planned to stop doing it, yet was reluctant to lose the lucrative income.

She then heard rumors that investors were making huge profits from warrants investments. Furthermore, Wang-er told her he knew a professional speculator who guaranteed profits. Sister Feng was tempted to try it out. Initially, she started with only $20,000 to $30,000. With a few trading successes and profits gained, she grew bolder and decided to use the household's monthly budget to speculate. However, good things don't last. Her bonds had depreciated in value and Sister Feng could not sell them without heavy losses. She paced anxiously in her room, realizing what the consequences would be if she was not able to hand out everyone's allowances.

Tan Chun entered her room at that moment. At a loss about what to do, Sister Feng told her what had happened. After listening, Tan Chun stamped her foot in anger. She said, "Sister Feng, you are too muddle-headed! There are vast differences between warrants and stocks. Warrants have financial leveraging effects. Even though speculators can make huge profits with limited capital, they can also suffer huge losses within a short period of time. How could you make such a reckless investment when you don't understand the factors affecting warrants trading and its prices?"

Sister Feng blushed in embarrassment and said, "I acted on the advice of an 'expert.'" Tan Chun asked for the background of this "expert" and then shook her head in disappointment, saying, "Yes, we should listen to expert advice when investing, but we should also determine if the person can be called an expert in the first place."

Hearing that, Sister Feng felt a deep sense of regret.

Read on to find out what happens.

HSBC Jintrust investment advisors recommend:

Don't be taken in by profit guarantees when investing

It is vital that one does not base investments on hearsay, especially the words of those who guarantee returns. One must remember that there is no free lunch in this world. If one seeks returns from investments, he or she must be able to bear the risks involved.

Chapter 6

Tan Chun Explains What an "Expert" is

Sister Feng Tells of Incurred Deficit

After putting half of the household's savings into investments in warrants that lost money, Sister Feng was explaining to Tan Chun that she had gotten into this plight because she had listened to the advice of an "expert." Tan Chun found it strange, however, as real experts would not make empty promises of gains and profits to customers, nor would they recommend products and packages that supposedly guaranteed no risk or losses.

To clarify the matter, Tan Chun pointed out that currently, the only kinds of investments that involve profits with no losses are bank deposits and Government bonds. If one wants higher profits, there will also be higher risk. Warrants are at the cutting edge of such risky investments, where huge returns can be reaped from small amounts, and huge losses are possible too. Tan Chun then added that the excessive claims made about those packages were false, but she was surprised that Sister Feng had actually believed them, and also had believed that the person who gave her the advice was an expert.

Sister Feng felt remorseful, and asked if Tan Chun had meant that people claiming to be experts were all cheats. Tan Chun replied that it was not necessarily the case, but one should be able to differentiate the experts from the fakes. She had learned through handling the $2 million in cash for her studies that it takes more than just verbal ability or the gift of the gab to be an expert. Tan Chun then explained that a financial consultant is equivalent to a scholar who, after studying, is still required to take specialized examinations such as the CFP, CFA, and CPA to prove his or her abilities.

Sister Feng paled in astonishment and went on to ask: "All these tests, they're definitely beyond the average person, but surely that's not all a person needs to know to actually do the job?"

Tan Chun continued to explain that to be a financial expert takes experience, not just knowledge from books and examinations. For instance, fund managers and financial advisors of fund management and insurance companies have all gained experience, having started out at the bottom before making it to the front line. Sister Feng then enquired if that would mean that Tan Chun and Sister Lin were experts, as they too had read the relevant books, as well as gained experience dealing in investments. But Tan Chun merely laughed, telling her that it takes more than just that to be a true expert. She used an analogy from the Chinese proverb: "The peony relies wholly on the presence of green leaves to bring out its beauty." A financial consultant also needs a team of financial analysts and researchers to help, through providing information ranging from the macroeconomics of the country and the movements of individual industries, to the performance and status of every particular bond and individual firm, changes in policies, interest rates, and capital flows. All of this would have been distilled from and based upon conclusions drawn from reading tens of thousands of reports, research, and analyses conducted by various local and international securities research institutes.

Sister Feng finally understood that it was impossible to be an expert without hard work and teamwork. She then questioned whether such experts were likely to be affordable to the average person. Tan Chun laughed and explained that this was far from the case. In fact, just a few thousand dollars invested in funds and financial products from banks and securities traders would warrant service levels no different from the "high rollers." You wouldn't have to spend your days scrutinizing the financial news or trying to track down inside information, as your expert would take over, managing all of your finances, selecting shares with the best investment potential, and helping you obtain the highest profits. Even all the mundane procedures involved in securities trading would be taken over by specialized personnel in the fund management companies, banks, and brokerages. When investing in funds, for example, to enjoy these services, one only has to pay the fund management company an annual fee of $15.

Tan Chun's words sent Sister Feng into a daze, but Ping-er, who was standing to the side, reminded them that the most important thing to do was to think of a way to recoup the losses and not go on talking about less urgent matters. Thus, Sister Feng panicked once more, saying that the household would all be waiting for their monthly allowances. Tan Chun concluded that since they had no choice, they might as well confess the whole truth to the matriarch, as it was about time the household made some changes. Without a budget or plan, spending more money would only lead to money shortages, and hence, it would require everyone's joint effort to get the household back on its feet. Sister Feng thought about Tan Chun's words and, feeling helpless with no alternatives, she kept quiet in consent.

After waiting for half the day at Wang Bao He and still not seeing the return of Sister Feng and company, the matriarch began to worry. After the dinner, Grandmother Jia went to look for Sister Feng in her room. Upon seeing Sister Feng, Grandmother asked, "What was all the fuss about leaving the restaurant in such a hurry?"

Sister Feng knelt down and cried in remorse, saying she knew how much the matriarch adored her and trusted her with the running of the household, but that she had failed her by making a mess of the situation. She was too ashamed to look at her. But seeing what was going on, the matriarch hurriedly asked Sister Feng what had actually happened. However, the crying Sister Feng was in no state to reply, so Tan Chun quickly told the story of how Sister Feng had made bad investments. Even though she was unhappy about the situation, the matriarch figured it wasn't the time to take her to task and merely said to Sister Feng that she knew of her loan-sharking, but reckoned that she knew what she was doing, and therefore had not mentioned it. However, now that they had had losses in the market, the matriarch decided to use the money from the family reserves, and asked Sister Feng about the amount of money still remaining. Hearing the matriarch's words, Sister Feng thought to herself that if she were to tell the truth, the matriarch might be worried. But if she kept mum about it, they might not even make it past a few days. She decided to come clean with every detail from the beginning.

Read on to find out what happened next.

HSBC Jintrust investment advisors recommend:

When making an investment, it is vital to heed the advice of an expert

But who is a real expert? Many accomplishments in a financial sector, vast combat experience with relevance to the specialized field, and a wide platform research base, coupled with the evidence of past achievements, make one an "investment expert." According to a statistic derived from "China's Report on Research Done on Fund Managers," which was conducted in April 2004, all of China's fund managers have an educational background of university level and above. Of those, 90 percent are master's degree holders. Their average experience in dealing with bonds is 7.7 years, so each candidate will have spent a vast 30,000 hours in this field! Apart from the individual experience accumulated, fund managers can also rely on the strength of research resources available—tens of thousands of research reports published by various local and international institutes, research on various major public companies done by established research professionals, internationally renowned investment analysis software and tools, and so on.

Hence, to leverage the expertise and resources of a real investment expert would greatly enhance one's chances of getting higher returns.

Chapter 7

No Plans are Made to Settle the Predicament

Tan Chun is Unfazed by Circumstances

When Grandmother Jia saw the latest account books, which were presented to her by Ping-er upon the request of Sister Feng, she realized that the income and expenditures did not tally and that the household was running a deficit.

Grandmother Jia anxiously stamped her foot, saying, "This is terrible! I always thought you would have a sense of control over the family. But now, we've actually eaten into next year's reserves and you still have the nerve to make senseless investments outside! These actions are going to ruin the family! How are we going to survive this?"

Sister Feng was too ashamed to utter a word. Tan Chun laughed, and said, "We can't blame Sister-in-law entirely for the sticky situation we are in. Grandmother Jia, how many people are actually competent to plan for their family? Sister-in-law was prompted to go into investments because she wanted to help with the daily expenditures of the family. After all, if it hadn't been for her resourcefulness, how would this family have survived till now?"

Upon hearing this, Grandmother Jia said, "You've got a point there! Indeed, it hasn't been easy on Sister Feng." Tan Chun said, "Let's organize a family meeting today, to put our heads together and come up with a feasible solution." With that, Grandmother Jia ordered her servant to ask Madam Wang, Li Wan, Bao Yu, Ying Chun, and Xi Chun to come in.

When everyone had assembled, Grandmother Jia broke the news to them that the finances of the family were fast depleting and things were currently very critical. She then asked, "Do any of you have any opinions regarding this issue?"

None of them had ever been through such a predicament before. All they knew was peace and happiness, with no hints of misery. Now they gazed at each other, not knowing what to do. As Grandmother Jia saw that they were of no help, she sighed. "Never would I have expected this day to befall the well-known Jia Clan!"

Tan Chun went up to her and said, "Grandmother Jia, I hope you will broaden your perspective. We can treat this whole issue as a turning point and take this chance to tidy up our family's finances, which is the first step in managing the family's wealth."

Grandmother Jia asked, "How do we go about that?" Tan Chun said, "We can create a balance sheet."

Bao Yu laughed and said, "To think Tan Chun has her moments of being muddle-headed! A balance sheet is used by public enterprises as a financial statement. How can we possibly implement it for family use?"

Tan Chun said, "Second Brother is the muddled one. You fail to realize that in order to plan for the future, it is vital that you understand the current circumstances. The starting point in managing the wealth within our family is to set up a balance sheet, to better understand our family's financial position."

Sister Feng enquired: "I keep track of the monthly accounts and record everything in the account book. Isn't that sufficient?"

Tan Chun explained: "Generally speaking, most people know the financial position of their family on a monthly basis. However, when it comes to the financial status of the family on a quarterly or yearly basis, it is not so obvious. Due to this lack of clarity, it is more difficult for one to understand the amount of risk that one is able to undertake when investing."

Sister Feng asked, "Do we need the assistance of an accountant in managing a balance sheet?"

Tan Chun said, "It isn't that difficult to tabulate, using a formula. The total assets of the family = liquid assets + investment assets + usage assets; the total liabilities of the family = short-term liabilities + long-term debt liabilities; the net assets of the family = total assets – total liabilities. The final net value is reflected in the net assets of the family. It also includes the family property accumulated over a period of time."

Before Tan Chun finished talking, Sister Feng clapped in agreement. "And you say it isn't difficult! After all that you've said, I've yet to understand anything."

Tan Chun said, "Sister-in-law, be patient. Let me explain. Liquid assets refer to currencies and bills, such as hard cash and demand deposits that can be readily converted; investment assets are investment currencies and bills that are long-term deposits, insurance, stocks, bonds, funds, futures, house and property investments, and collections that are maintained for the purpose of preserving and increasing value; usage assets refer to assets designated for private use, such as housing, furniture, transportation, books, clothes, food, and various other commodities."

Sister Feng laughed. "I do understand now. Short-term liabilities refer to debts which must be repaid within a short span of time, namely, within a year?"

Tan Chun laughed and said, "Sister-in-law is really intelligent, and a fast learner. Long-term liabilities refer to debts which must be repaid over a longer period, namely, after a year."

Sister Feng said, "Forget about the praise already; from this day on, I'll never claim to be intelligent again."

For further details, refer to the following chapter.

HSBC Jintrust investment advisors recommend:

The first step in the planning of a family's finances is to set up a balance sheet

Understanding the family's financial position is the starting point of a financial journey toward wealth. Without healthy financials, there is no basis for any wonderful future financial plans.

In order to grasp a family's financial status, one can make use of the rationale behind the corporate balance sheet—that is, to list the assets of the family and the liabilities and debts, and to do the following analysis. Firstly, one must compare one's salary and one's liabilities to determine a personal debt ratio. Should one's debt ratio exceed a certain limit, then there will be cause for worry. One must decrease one's personal liabilities to prevent stress resulting from debts. (Based on the general rule of thumb, this limit should not exceed 70 percent.) Secondly, seek to have a balance of long-, mid-, and short-term debts based on repayment periods and one's ability to repay. This is to avoid lumping various repayment periods and deadlines together so that one is unable to repay the entire amount when all the debts become due at the same time.

Chapter 8

Plans are Made to Revive the Clan

Bao Chai Discusses Family Funds

Grandmother Jia, anxious about the depletion of the family's property, called for a family meeting. Tan Chun said that it was important first to set up a balance sheet to ascertain the total amount of family assets. Sister Feng reached for a calculator and calculated the assets, based on the formula provided by Tan Chun. She spoke in dismay: "We've yet to reach the trough in which we have negative assets. However, the debt ratio has reached over 90 percent, which is far greater than the limit that enterprises set for themselves."

Tan Chun continued: "You've yet to hear the worst. All of our debts are due to be paid off at around the same time, and the deadlines to clear them are nearing. Soon enough, our debtors will be knocking on our door." Everyone was shocked at this news, and young Xi Chun was so overwhelmed she broke down in tears.

Tan Chun spoke up quickly: "What has come over all of you? What's important now is to come up with a feasible solution to overcome the problem. No point in fretting." Upon hearing this, the crowd calmed down. Tan Chun continued: "Understanding the family's financial position is the first step in wealth management. We must ascertain the current status of the family's finances and establish 'where we are.' It is then vital to come up with financial goals to define 'where we're going.'"

Sister Feng said, "Tan Chun, you are so knowledgable. Set a financial goal for us."

Tan Chun said, "From what I see, we've been spending too lavishly, and our income is minimal. We have been relying solely on the income of the men in the family and on the rental fees that we receive from the country property. Small income, coupled with great expenditures, is the cause of the financial predicament that we now face. Let's split up the finances. Both Eldest Sister-in-law and Second Sister-in-law have their own families, and the siblings are old enough to be independent. Every family can then make monthly contributions to Grandmother for rent and groceries, and take that opportunity to visit her more often to do our bit of filial duty."

Sister Feng sighed. "I've had that idea for a while, but I didn't want to say it."

Tan Chun laughed. "I'm a straightforward person, and I don't have any qualms about what I say. In any case, I'll be leaving for America soon, and I don't have any worry that people will blame me behind my back."

Grandmother Jia said, "The people here aren't the muddle-headed, jealous sort. I think the idea that Tan Chun came up with is great, since it's in the interest of everyone. How do you feel about it?"

The group agreed. "It is a change for the better, and we should have done it earlier." However, Bao Chai had reservations regarding the idea, saying, "There is still one issue that we didn't take into consideration. The risks are very high with everyone embarking on a new route. Should unforeseen circumstances arise, such as sickness or the loss of jobs, on whom can we depend?"

Grandmother Jia nodded in agreement, saying, "Bao Chai's worries are not unfounded. Should everyone just bother with their own needs, not only will we become more mercenary and inconsiderate, but wouldn't it also be unbecoming of a clan like ours? Suppose each family contributed $3,000, and we pulled the funds together to form a risk fund. With that, we would be able to fall back on our pooled reserves should a predicament arise for any particular family in the household."

Everyone responded: "Agreed."

Tan Chun said, "Since Bao Chai came up with such a brilliant idea, it's only right that she be in charge of it."

Bao Chai said, "That should not be the case! As the saying goes, 'The capable undertake more.' Of course, it's Sister Feng who should manage the fund."

Sister Feng spoke hurriedly: "How can I still be qualified to handle financial stuff? From now on, I'd rather be a manual worker and wait on Grandmother Jia, yes Mother-in-law?"

Grandmother Jia said, "Do you all treat this as just another ordinary assignment? Dodging back and forth! We cannot afford to run a deficit. In fact, for each year, there should be a continuous positive rate of return. There is no room for a single error. Bao Chai, please stop declining. We cannot have anything untoward happen in the future!" With that, Bao Chai accepted the task.

Bao Yu laughed. "It's all Tan Chun's fault. As of tomorrow, even I will have to head out to work."

Bao Chai declared, "From today on, not only do we need to formulate a financial goal, but also reform our life goals!"

Dai Yu added, "Exactly. It's not only a matter of setting right one's financial goals, but also resetting one's life goals!"

Tan Chun said, "If this happens, it's for the good of the Jia clan."

To find out what Tan Chun said next, go to the following chapter.

HSBC Jintrust investment advisors recommend:

The second step in wealth management within a family is to set a financial goal

A clear investment goal is vital in ascertaining the investment horizon and strategy. If you are 30 years old at present and your goal is to enjoy a carefree retirement life after the age of 60, then the timeframe for this investment will be at least 30 years. With an

investment goal, the timeframe for your investment will be clear. Of course, the goal of investing just to raise one's retirement income is not sufficient. An investment goal must be precise, down to dollar amounts that one would foresee oneself needing to have his or her desired retirement lifestyle.

Chapter 9

The Young Master Awakes to Ponder His Future

The Young Mistress Sets Off to Fulfill Her Dreams

It was said that after the Jia clan held a meeting and evaluated their assets, they adopted Tan Chun's suggestion of distributing their finances, with each family setting up its own home and determining its family's own financial goals.

Grandmother Jia said, "Now that it has come to this, we might as well steel our hearts and split the family property. Besides, what is left now is very limited. Once Sister Feng has done the tallying, we shall distribute the money to each of you. With this small start-up fund, every one of you will do your own planning to fulfill your own financial goals."

Tan Chun said, "The purpose of ascertaining family property is to know our financial position, or 'where we are,' and then decide on a goal so that we will know what our next step should be, or 'where to go.' The next important thing is to know how to get to our destination. Now that the splitting of our family property is done, each individual family's situation, financial burdens, lifestyles, and risk-taking limits will be vastly different from one another. Everyone's target and financial management solutions will vary. From now on, everyone will have nothing more than his or her own resources, and will be left to prove his or her own worth."

Upon hearing this, they all lowered their heads and started mumbling, before dispersing.

All the drawers and cupboards were overturned in the Jia household as the various assets were organized, distributed, or auctioned off, and everyone was thrown into a frenzy. Only Bao Yu, who was used to a life filled with comfort and ease, did nothing. He stood by looking at his family in chaos because of the haggling over property.

One day, he walked over to the Xiao Xiang Chamber, only to see Dai Yu sitting on her bed wiping away tears. He asked, "Who made you angry this time, little sister?"

She sobbed and replied, "Who's angry? I'm only thinking about my future!"

Surprised, Bao Yu asked, "Why were you thinking so far into the future for no reason?"

Dai Yu replied, "Now every family is living by themselves. My parents have both passed on. With no one to rely on, what am I going to do from now on?"

Bao Yu laughed. "No matter what happens, you'll still have me around! What do you have to worry about?"

Dai Yu blushed and said, "There you go again, with nothing proper to say! Enough about me. Talk about yourself—you'll have to be more prudent. If not, you just might be poor in the future!"

"Sister Feng just gave me a $2 million distribution. Granny later secretly passed me many jewels. So how will that not be enough for us to spend?"

Dai Yu said, "Of course that's not enough! You always underestimate your financial needs. Do you know how much it costs just for your sister to study overseas? She's attending Harvard University. Every school year will cost about $24,000. Her food and rental expenses will be about $8,000. Not forgetting her living expenditures, her Bachelor's degree will cost your family $1.4 million. And what if your child wants to attend Harvard in the future?"

Bao Yu answered stiffly, "Don't I already have $10 million? What do I have to worry about?"

Dai Yu poked him gently on his head and said, "How could you have forgotten about the inflation that Granny mentioned yesterday? School fees will rise along with inflation anywhere, including in America, where college fees have been growing at double-digit rates, and overtaking inflation by far. In 10 years, even $3 million will not be enough!"

Intimidated, Bao Yu asked, "Do I really need that much?"

Dai Yu uttered a "humph" and continued: "There is more that you are ignorant of than you know. From January 1, 2006 onward, every individual's pension account contribution was adjusted from 8 percent to 11 percent of his or her income. This will have a greater impact on people of our generation. Do you really think that solely relying on a pension for retirement is going to be enough to sustain us?"

Bao Yu hesitated. "So you mean that I'll have to depend on my own personal savings for our old age?"

"Isn't that what I said? If you still don't start planning now, in the future I'll . . ." Dai Yu swallowed in mid-sentence, then used her handkerchief to hide her face.

Bao Yu was staring blankly into space when he noticed Tan Chun enter. "So there you are! This makes everything easier."

Bao Yu asked her what she was talking about, and Tan Chun replied, "I'm here to bid farewell. I've already bought the airplane ticket, and I will set out tomorrow."

Shocked, Bao Yu pulled on Tan Chun and said, "What's the urgency? I was just about to ask you about financial planning!"

Tan Chun smiled. "Even if you were to ask me right now, you can't expect me to have all the right answers for you. Wait until I'm back from my studies, then I'll be able to help each and every one of you plan." Defeated, Bao Yu had no choice but to lay the matter to rest.

The next day, Tan Chun bade farewell to everybody else, and boarded her flight.

More will be explained in the following chapter.

HSBC Jintrust investment advisors recommend:

The third step in the planning of a family's finances is to create a financial plan

After agreeing on a goal, setting up an action plan comes next. For example, if your goal is to accumulate $3 million in retirement savings in 30 years, and if the annual rate of return for the year is 8 percent, then you have to invest $2,013 every month; if the annual rate of return rises to 10 percent, then you should invest $1,327 every month; if the annual rate of return reaches 15 percent, then the month's investment will drop to $433. You can weigh the differences in returns and risks of different types of investments, and choose an investment plan best suited to your goals.

Chapter 10

Leng Zi Xing Talks Animatedly About the New Red Chamber

Jia Tan Chun is Surprised by the Big Difference When She Comes Home

Tan Chun left for Harvard University in America to pursue advanced studies. After four years, she managed to attain the qualifications to be a financial planner, financial analyst, and so on. But as she had not been in contact with her family during that period of time, she was very concerned. When her graduation ceremony ended, she quickly packed her luggage and bought an airplane ticket home.

When waiting at the airport in New York, she suddenly saw a man walking toward her, saying, "What a coincidence!"

Tan Chun looked at him carefully, and realized that he was actually the general manager of Jin Ling Antique Company, Leng Zi Xing. Leng Zi Xing was a very active and well-traveled person. Tan Chun had visited his antique shop before, and that was how she had gotten to know him. Leng Zi Xing was always full of praise for Tan Chun for being a girl who was extraordinarily capable. Now that he had met an old friend in a distant land, he was overjoyed, pulling Tan Chun aside and flooding her with questions. Tan Chun found out that Leng Zi Xing had just come from China, and asked him immediately, "Do you know anything about how my family's been?"

Sighing, Leng Zi Xing said, "Granny Jia is still holding it against me for criticizing the Jias. She stopped letting me call a long time ago. How am I to know what's going on in the Jia house?"

Tan Chun smiled. "Don't lie. You're the most informed person in the whole capital. What do you not know?"

This time, Leng Zi Xing smiled too, and said, "Now that your clan has gone through some revolutionary changes, they have made news throughout the entire capital! Even the people on the street know. In fact, your clan ought to thank me. If Granny Jia hadn't heard me say that people in your family did not know how to plan their wealth, they wouldn't have had you learn financial planning, nor would your family finances have been split, and they wouldn't have known how to live independently."

"Don't beat around the bush now; quickly tell me what changes have happened in my family."

Leng Zi Xing replied, "Don't be in such a hurry. Let's find a place to sit down. I'll explain then."

Tan Chun had no choice but to be patient and she followed Leng Zi Xing into Starbucks just beside them. After they ordered two cups of coffee, the chat started to warm up.

Leng Zi Xing said, "Your sisters have all started to show considerable prospects now. Let's talk about your Second Sister-in-law. She has established a 'Grand View Garden Tourism Limited Company,' and made the Grand Garden the most famous tourist spot in the capital. She has become one of the city's most successful career women, and was even on the cover of *Celebrity* magazine."

As he was speaking, he removed a magazine from his briefcase and handed it to Tan Chun. Indeed, on the cover was a picture of Sister Feng smiling back at her, with her youthful appearance belying the authority she commanded.

Tan Chun said, "Sister Feng has always been a leading figure among the ladies. This is not unexpected. What about the others?"

He replied, "There are other famous people in the clan. Lin Dai Yu is now one of the hottest female Internet authors around. Her book of poetry, *Poems of the Flowers' Burial*, has sold out, with online blog hits of tens of millions!"

Marveling at this news, Tan Chun asked, "Why is Sister Lin's blog so popular?"

Leng Zi Xing smiled and said, "Because everyone's curious as to how her relationship with Bao Yu will advance. Oh, and there's another one that you wouldn't guess—that is your Fourth Sister Xi Chun. She is now a painter enjoying a considerable amount of fame. Her 'Memories of the Grand Garden' has caught the eye of many art galleries. They are fighting to purchase the painting, and that has also resulted in the increased popularity of the Grand Garden. There are also Xue Bao Chai and Shi Xiang Yun, who have been called 'White Bone Elite.'"

Surprised, Tan Chun asked, "Why is that so?"

Leng Zi Xing laughed. "White collar workers, the backbone of the company, and the elites of society!"

Tan Chun laughed with him and said, "It's good to know that my sisters are all standing on their own two feet. What about Second Brother?"

Leng Zi Xing sighed. "Bao Yu still has not changed from his old habits, still preferring to hang around with the girls, working in fits and starts, and lacking perseverance."

Tan Chun could not help but furrow her brow upon hearing this.

Leng Zi Xing then asked Tan Chun, "So what did our Third Missy learn from studying overseas?"

She replied, "My greatest achievement has been to learn how to manage my finances while studying abroad. I have been trying to reduce expenditures, such as by buying second-hand clothes, and renting inexpensive apartments that are further away from school but still accessible. I have also been racking my brain over how to raise my income. In fact, I have been working temporary jobs since the second semester of school. I also bought money market funds with the money meant for later years of study, and even used the profits gained to dabble in the American stock markets just before my return. Managing my finances while studying abroad has not only let me lead a more comfortable lifestyle, but more importantly, it has also trained me to plan for my life."

Leng Zi Xing grinned. "Third Missy is right. Now that there are many more people studying overseas at their own expense, these students have to learn to be careful about how to save and make money." He continued: "Now that you are an expert at managing finances, you can show your mettle when you return home."

After chatting for a while more, they both went their own ways. For further details, please go to the next chapter.

HSBC Jintrust investment advisors recommend:

Learn how to manage your wealth even when studying abroad

Rational management of wealth not only helps people who study abroad to handle their situation with ease, but it also prevents the predicament of not having enough money when spending is warranted. In addition, it trains and improves one's ability to manage one's own life. Academic achievements and economic conditions are tightly linked. Studying abroad not only gives you an academic education, but, more importantly, it also lets you decide your own destiny!

Chapter 11

Li Wan Complains Tearfully About Financial Records

Tan Chun Explains About Life Cycles

When Tan Chun returned to her country, she was finally able to go back home. Everyone welcomed her back, seeing her looking fresh and youthful, and better than before. She was silently assessing her sisters, whose conduct had changed: Dai Yu had become all the more graceful; Bao Chai, on the other hand, was more poised; but Bao Yu remained as childish as ever, fooling around with the girls as always.

They sat down and did some catching up. Tan Chun recounted the meeting she had had with Leng Zi Xing, and congratulated everyone on their individual achievements. Only Li Wan furrowed her brow and kept silent.

Everyone asked if she was troubled that her work was not proceeding smoothly, but Li Wan said, "I'm not very concerned about work, whether I have achievements or not. All I want is to have enough to bring Lan-er up. However, this money management thing is making my head ache. Didn't you buy some money market funds before leaving for America? I had thought that it was a good idea, as the profit was higher than those bank fixed deposits, and they didn't have much risk of loss. So I used all the money I saved every month and invested in funds like those, in the hope of saving up for Lan-er's college fees in 10 years."

Upon hearing this, Sister Feng put her palms together, saying, "Wow, so our Eldest Sister-in-law has already learned how to manage her money too!"

But Li Wan just gave a long sigh. "These funds may be good, but they only give about 2 percent return per annum. In these four years, they haven't even kept up with inflation. The money is worth less, yet education fees are skyrocketing."

Bao Yu suggested, "You could buy some shares. They have gone up 30 percent this year. Isn't that a good way to increase your wealth?"

Li Wan said, "I'd heard about that, too—that the stock market has been like a gold mine, and that anyone can profit from it. That was why I hurriedly went and changed the money market funds for stock funds." Tears started to roll down her cheeks as she finished, "But how was I to know that after I bought the shares, the market would start to fall like a brick? How am I going to send Lan-er to college this way?"

Everybody looked at Tan Chun, hoping for reassurance. Tan Chun asked for someone to bring some water, and got Li Wan to wash her face and touch up her make-up. She spoke sincerely: "Well, I don't think that Eldest Sister-in-law should be too worried. This money won't be used for 10 years. Just as the stock market has fallen now, who's to know if it will go up tomorrow?"

Everybody nodded. Li Wan stopped crying. She asked, "Then was my decision to dabble in the stock market right?"

Tan Chun did not answer, but laughed. "When I entered the house, I saw Lan-er and a few of his boy servants playing soccer in the yard. Only a few years have passed, and his skills have certainly improved. However, Second Master Lian, on the other hand, used to love playing soccer, but I heard that he now prefers to play tennis."

Sister Feng said, "That's normal. As one ages, the strength to run around a whole field decreases."

Tan Chun clapped her hands together. "That's right. After a decade, maybe Second Master Lian might turn to playing golf or something else. As people grow older, their strength will inevitably decrease. When your life enters a new stage, the type of sports suitable for you will change. Investments are no different; they also have the problem of relevance in our life cycles. When we get older, our investment period will not be as long as it was, and the amount of risk we can take on will decline. Correspondingly, the investments we make will have to be more conservative. That is why someone like Eldest Sister-in-law, who wants to plan for Lan-er's education fund, has to plan according to the amount of risk that she can bear. The time limit of her investments will go through changes, and she should have a 10-year plan."

Everybody gasped with admiration for Tan Chun upon hearing this, and asked more about how to make a 10-year plan.

To find out how Tan Chun was going to help Li Wan with the planning of Lan-er's education fund, please read the next chapter.

HSBC Jintrust investment advisors recommend:

In different phases of life, you should have different investment combinations

With the passage of time, usually a person's ability to bear risk will decline. That is why the choice of investments should gradually become more conservative. Young investors (20 to 30 years old) are able to bear higher risks, so in their investment portfolios, they can hold a higher proportion of liquid investment products with higher risk, and less products such as bonds. For investors in their prime phase (30 to 50 years), cash mobility for that period may be adequate, but financial burdens will have increased. That is why they should consider mid- to long-term (investment periods of above three years) risk-type products, and still maintain fair liquidity of investments of a bond nature. For older investors (50 years old and above), controlling the risk will be the primary consideration; they should consider investing more in bonds, and less in riskier products of more than a three years investment period.

There is another very simple and easy rule for investment port-folios, called the "100 investment law"—that is, "The proportion of risky investments in an investment portfolio = 100 − age." Deduct your age from 100; that should be the proportion of risky investments, such as stocks, that you can have in your portfolio. For example, a 30-year-old man can have 70 percent of his investments in shares; when he reaches 60 years old, his stock proportion should be adjusted lower to 40 percent.

Chapter 12

Loving Mother Plans for Son's Education Fees

Son is Frugal with Basic Expenses

Li Wan was asking Tan Chun how to plan for Lan-er's education fees.

Tan Chun said, "It'll be 10 years before Lan-er attends college. You'll have to do a 10-year investment plan. During the first five years, your investment period is still considered long, so your ability to take on risk is much higher. Therefore you can invest half of your assets in stocks. The next five years, the time before Lan-er attends college will be shorter, and you'll have to gradually become more conservative in your investments. That is why the proportion you invest in stocks will have to be less; investments in bonds will have to be higher instead. If the funds that you buy in the beginning are purely equity funds, you'll have to consider converting to bond funds and money market funds as the investment period shortens."

Li Wan frowned. "Doesn't that mean the rate of return will be lower?"

Sister Feng interjected: "You're just thinking about the returns. Don't forget, the risk you'll be taking will also be less!"

Tan Chun said, "Sister Feng is still the same, as shrewd as always."

Sister Feng smiled. "Of course, I am famous for calculating after all! I still remember that year when all of you wanted to set up the Poetry Club, asking for money from me. Didn't Sister-in-law say that I was a stingy and number-crunching block-head then?"

Even Li Wan was unable to suppress her laughter. "Did you guys hear that? She can still remember things that happened such a long time ago!"

Sister Feng clapped her hands and said, "All right! I'll forget all about that episode with this laughter of yours!"

Everybody laughed. Li Wan knew that Sister Feng was saying that to help cheer her up, and she said, "Of course, I understand that our investments should be adjusted in line with our age, but after all, I am not a professional. I don't understand complicated things like when to change investment products, or what kind of investment products to change to. When the time comes, I'll be like every other person, getting enthusiastic when I see the stock market rally, and panicking when it deflates. Ultimately, I'm just chasing trends!"

Tan Chun said, "You're not wrong. Greed and fear are just like Second Brother's jade stone. They're two qualities that everybody is born with. They are really hard to overcome. That is why, even though everyone knows the rationales behind investments, not many can really carry them out."

"Does that mean there is no solution to the problem?" Li Wan asked.

"That may not necessarily be the case. During the years when I was abroad, I found out that foreigners have started to take a fancy to a kind of 'life-cycle fund.' These kinds of investments will be able to help investors overcome certain human weaknesses."

Curious, Sister Feng asked, "Why such a weird name? It sounds like they're completely different from other specialty funds!"

"The reason they are named that way is that the investment combinations they provide are able to satisfy the investor's needs at different phases of their lives. This kind of fund will usually have a fixed target period. The fund's investment combination will adjust itself according to the period approaching the goal's deadline. The further away the deadline is, the higher the proportion of riskier investments. And when nearing the deadline, it will gradually increase the proportion of lower risk investments. This is particularly suited for the individual investor's savings for old age or children's education funds, with the characteristics of decreasing risk tolerance and shortening investment periods."

Sister Feng nodded. "I understand now. Eldest Sister-in-law will have to choose a life-cycle fund with a target of 10 years for Lan-er's college fees 10 years from now."

Tan Chun pointed out: "No wonder Eldest Sister-in-law said that your heart and mind have the clarity of crystals. You are indeed intelligent to grasp concepts so quickly."

As they were speaking, a perspiring Lan-er ran in, burying his head in his mother's embrace. Li Wan wiped off the perspiration from his forehead and said, "Look at your jersey. Why do you still wear it even when it's so worn out? I'll take you to buy a new one tomorrow."

Jia Lan shook his head and said, "No, it's okay. This shirt's still fine; I can still wear it another two years."

Everyone heard, and praised him: "Good boy, you already know how to be frugal at such a young age. You really do live up to your mother's expectations."

To learn Jia Lan's reply, please read on.

HSBC Jintrust investment advisors recommend:

A very effective and simple "Lazy man's investment method" is investment in life-cycle funds

Life-cycle funds have been the recent rage among common funds overseas. This kind of bond usually has a target period, and the nearer it is to the target period, the more conservative the bond's investment combination will be. The proportion of stock funds in the combination will gradually decrease, while investments with fixed returns will gradually increase. After reaching its target period, investments will be converted to various money market funds or low-risk bond funds. This is to ensure that the investor's wealth will not be exposed to too much risk from then on. From the year 1996 to 2004, the market size of life-cycle funds grew from US$6 billion to US$103 billion. The compounded annual rate of growth has reached a stunning 43 percent, and has been said to have the highest rate of growth for common funds.

HSBC Jintrust 2016 Lifecycle Fund is a 10-year target period life-cycle fund. The fund will adjust its proportion of stock investments every year. Nearing the year 2016, the upper limit of the proportion of shares will be lowered, and the lower limit of proportion of bonds will be raised. After the year 2016, it will be a low-risk fund that mainly invests in short- to mid-term bonds and money market tools. For parents who are about 30 to 45 years in age, their children are still studying in elementary school and

junior high, and they will need money for their children's college education about 10 years later. That is why the 2016 Lifecycle Fund is suitable for these parents, who need to start raising money for their children's education fees. For investors who are above 45 years old, the 2016 Lifecycle Fund is an investment tool that can help them prepare for old age and future medical expenses.

Chapter 13

Little Boy Draws Favor with Lavish Gift

Pampered Girl Attracts Scolding by Asking for Allowance

I t was said that everyone was praising Jia Lan for being sensible; however, Jia Lan took out a silk embroidered box and gave it to Li Wan. Li Wan asked, "What is this?" and opened the box. The inside was lined with crepe silk, on top of which lay a pearl necklace, bright and dazzling to the eye. Jia Lan said, "Mother, perhaps you have forgotten, today is Mother's Day. I have bought this specially for you." Li Wan heard this and was shocked instead of being happy. She said, "My son, where did you get the money to buy this?"

Jia Lan replied, "From my daily savings, of course."

Li Wan said, "I don't believe it. I don't give you so much for your yearly red packet. How could it be enough to buy these things? I know you're lying."

Jia Lan hurriedly said, "It is truly bought from my allowance. You don't know, mother—the yearly red packets that you, grand-dad, and grandma gave me, I changed them all into gold coins and saved them in my piggy bank. I heard from Second Uncle recently that the price of gold has appreciated, so I begged him to help me sell my gold coins. That is how I got the money to buy the pearl necklace. If you don't believe me, you can check with Second Uncle."

Bao Yu immediately spoke up. "I really was the one who helped him change his gold coins for money. It's hard to blame him for being so generous at such a young age."

Li Wan said, "Oh, if that's the case, then so be it, but why spend the money?" Even as she said it, her heart was joyous. She pulled Jia Lan into her embrace, remembering the early death of her husband and the hardship of her lone struggle with her son. Unable to hold back, her tears suddenly fell, and she quickly rubbed them away. Everyone in the room looked at the touching scene and felt a sense of sadness.

Sister Feng asked, "Sister, how did you teach Brother Lan to be so sensible?"

Li Wan replied, "Ever since he was young, I taught him that money doesn't come easy. I even specially brought him along to my workplace, just to let him experience the hardship of earning money. Jia Lan has known how to do accounting ever since he was 10. Every week, I let him draw up a simple weekly expenditure plan. This way, he can understand the house-hold's overhead and expenditure situation. Through accounting, I find that Jia Lan has become more systematic and particular about details."

Tan Chun piped up: "This is the way things should be. When I was in America, I found that the foreigners also inculcate financial education in their children at a tender age. Parents are teaching their children at the age of three the difference between coins and notes; at the age of four, the children learn the value of the different coins and what they can buy with them; at five, they are told where money comes from; at six, they learn how to count money; at seven, they learn how to read price tags, and at eight, they know how to save money in a bank. . ."

Sister Feng exclaimed, "I only knew that you have to start young when learning computers, but I never thought that you have to start early with financial education as well! Lan's sister Qiao has been brought up like a precious phoenix by her parents, maid, and grandmother, and hence, only knows how to live the good life, unlike her brother."

As she said it, someone shouted from the outside, "I'm home from school!" A girl dressed in flower-patterned silk breezed into the room.

Tan Chun, seeing upon closer inspection that it was Qiao Jie, smiled and said, "After not seeing you for a few years, I find you've grown much prettier."

Sister Feng scolded: "Your aunt just returned from America, and you don't even know to greet her first? Such insolence!"

Qiao Jie hurriedly smiled and greeted her. She leaned on Sister Feng lazily and said mischievously, "Mother, I saw the latest MP3 player today and I love it. Give me some money!"

Sister Feng said sternly, "You have countless MP3 players and yet you're still not satisfied. I'm afraid in the future, even all of our family's wealth won't be enough to fund your spending."

Qiao Jie saw that her mother was not in her usual mood and lost interest. She caught sight of Jia Lan standing at the side and hurried over to chat with him.

Off to the side, Sister Feng said to Tan Chun, "Now that you have seen it too, this daughter of mine, how should I teach her?"

If you want to know what reply Tan Chun gave, you will have to read the next chapter.

HSBC Jintrust investment advisors recommend:

Financial management education must span your child's entire development

Apart from paying attention to a child's intelligence quotient and emotional quotient, has it ever occurred to you that the level of a child's "financial quotient" might change his or her whole life? Financial management education must start from an early age and must span a child's development. As a child grows up, parents must help him or her understand different financial concepts. For example, children aged 5 to 7 years old must understand the different sources that money comes from, and know the various uses of money; children aged 7 to 11 years old must learn how to manage their own money, recognizing how savings can be used to meet future needs; students aged 11 to 14 years old must understand the factors that affect people's expenditures and savings, and know how to improve their personal financial capacity; 14- to 16-year-old students must learn how to use some financial tools and services, including how to commence with budgeting and savings.

Give a man a fish and he will eat for a day. Teach him how to fish and he will eat for a lifetime. Letting your children develop good financial habits is more important than helping them manage their finances.

(For further information on financial education, please log on to the HSBC fund management company Web site http://www.hsbcjt.cn.)

Chapter 14

Sister Feng Seeks Financial Education

Tan Chun Discusses a Regular Investment Plan

Sister Feng was asking for advice from Tan Chun on how to teach her daughter Qiao Jie. Tan Chun said, "Theoretically, you still have to have a hand in this. If you don't get involved, you won't know what will happen in the future when she leaves your side."

Sister Feng said, "How could I not know to keep an eye on her? She's my only child and her body is fragile. Being strict with her could harm her. Hence, I have spoiled her." She could not help sighing as she said it.

Tan Chun said, "From what I've seen from your girl's attitude toward money, the biggest problem seems to be 'unlimited access.' In America, statistics show that the more money children receive from their parents, the less accumulated savings children have; on the other hand, the less money children receive from their parents, the more they accumulate. Therefore, we can see that parents' gifts will more often than not cause children not to practice the managing of finances, and so they will find it hard to be financially independent. With regard to children like Qiao Jie, the first and most important thing that you must learn to say is 'no.' Firmly reject any unreasonable requests." Sister Feng heard this and nodded her head repeatedly.

Tan Chun said, "Teaching Qiao Jie how to spend money is only the first step in financial education. You still have to teach her how to earn money. The monthly allowance that you give Qiao Jie is actually the best tool to help her practice her financial management skills. You should teach her how to divide it rationally. She can use a portion for her own expenditures such as buying makeup and other things, another portion should be for her investments, and so on."

Sister Feng heard this and asked immediately, "But what kind of investments should we make?"

Tan Chun replied, "You can go to the bank and begin a regular investing plan under her name. Let her buy some of the funds every month and accumulate money over a period of time. She will realize that the returns from investments are good."

Grandmother Jia frowned and said, "Buy funds every month? Isn't that the same as depositing small amounts and then withdrawing a lump sum? It was the fad for a while when I was young. But nowadays, the bank interest rates are so low, who would be foolish enough to still faithfully deposit sums in the bank every month? Who'd think that there are moments where our Tan Chun's talents are exhausted too!"

Tan Chun said, "Granny, allow me to explain. Drawing up a regular investment plan, depositing small amounts, and then withdrawing a lump sum may seem to be the same—that investors draw a fixed amount from their bank accounts every month. But depositing small amounts and then withdrawing a lump sum only uses this sum of money for savings. On the other hand, a regular investment plan uses this money to buy designated funds. They, in reality, unify the savings and investment functions. Due to the function of compound interest, the small sum of monthly investments, accumulating little by little, will become a large sum of money. Take, for example, our country's 1998–2005 stock fund, inclusive of hybrid funds' yearly average return ratio of 8.49 percent. Even if you only invest $200 every month, if you persevere for 42 years, you can become a millionaire!"

Grandmother Jia nodded. "This is it, and a regular investment plan can achieve the effect of 'collecting sand to build towers.'"

Sister Feng continued: "They can also help Qiao Jie nurture the good habit of regular investment."

Tan Chun said, "The benefits of a regular fund investing plan don't just end here. When the market price comes down, you can buy more, and when the market price goes up, you can buy less. This is because no matter how the market price fluctuates, you always regularly invest a fixed amount in the fund. When the fund's net worth increases, this fixed amount of money will buy a smaller number of units. However, when the fund's net worth decreases, more units can be bought. If you accumulate for many years, investment costs and risk will naturally decrease."

Sister Feng clapped and said, "This is so very simple. We don't have to be troubled by choosing the best time to enter the market." The fact is that ever since being greatly disappointed by her failed investments in warrants, Sister Feng had had a lingering fear of timing. Sister Feng liked this "investment for dummies."

Sister Feng thought and asked: "Qiao Jie's monthly allowance can be used to invest in funds regularly. Then what about me? If I have a large sum of saved up capital now, should I do lump sum investments or regular fixed investments?"

If you want to know what Tan Chun's reply was, you will have to read the next chapter.

HSBC Jintrust investment advisors recommend:

Cultivate the habit of regular investment

What could you do if you were given $100 monthly? Go to a restaurant? Buy a pair of shoes? Your $100 would soon be used up. Have you ever thought that if you save this $100 every month, you might just become a millionaire?

If a fixed $100 is invested every month into a particular fund (namely, a regular fund investing plan), then, if the fund's yearly average return ratio reaches 15 percent and you can persevere for 35 years, the value of investment return that you should be getting will reach $1.47 million.

Why is this so? Because of the time value effect of compound interest, the snowball effect of regular investment is easy to see. The small monthly investment will begin to accumulate a small sum and will then turn into a large sum of money. Many people fail to recognize how powerful the effects of habit are. A good habit may bring you pleasant surprises, and it may even change your life! Furthermore, making regular investments avoids the problem of timing. To most investors who are unable to time investments precisely, this is a simple and effective mid-term or long-term investment strategy.

Chapter 15

Sister Feng Gains
Insight into Investment

*Tan Chun Advises Investing Early and not to
be Overly Concerned with Timing*

It was said that Tan Chun discussed at great length the benefits
of a regular fund investment plan. Sister Feng's confidence
was restored and she quickly inquired of Tan Chun, "If there
is a large sum of laid-up capital, should we choose a one-time
investment of the whole amount or regular investing?"

Tan Chun said, "If the fund investment market is on the up-
trend, then it would be favorable for a one-time, or lump sum,
investment. On the other hand, if the market is in its correction
phase, then a regular fund investment plan would effectively spread
out the risks via the cost-averaging effect. As for the China market,
under the trends of sustained economic development, it is expected

to rise in the long run. Only during short periods will there be adjustments and reverses."

Sister Feng heard this and said, "Doesn't that mean single sum investment is better? I am the sort of person who would rather 'hit the golden chime once, than hit the broken drum 3,000 times.' One-time investment is still more nimble and efficient!"

Tan Chun shook her head and said, "But don't forget the advantage of a regular fund investment plan, which can lower risks. There are two kinds of investment strategies that complement each other. The one-time lump sum investment may be used for current fund storage management, whereas the regular fund investment plan will be used to manage future regular investments. As long as there is a medium- or long-term goal for managing finances, you can use both lump sum investment and regular investment to realize your goals. You can first use your capital on hand to purchase funds using the lump sum method, and then make it a point from then on to take out a certain amount from each month's income for regular investment. Sister Feng has plenty of money now, with much income every month. I even heard when I was overseas that Sister Feng has already made it into the ranking of 'China's richest people.' Lump sum investing coupled with a regular fund investment plan is most appropriate." These words made Sister Feng beam with joy.

Sister Feng asked again, "Then what kind of funds should I choose for regular investment?"

Tan Chun replied, "You should pay attention to fund companies that have rich experience in investing, and invest in those that are stable. As for the types of funds, if you use the method of fixed investment with those stock funds that have great fluctuations, you will be able to see the effects of lowered risk with this method."

Sister Feng heard this and nodded repeatedly; she rose immediately to set out to buy funds. However, Bao Yu said, "Sister Feng, don't be so hasty. These days, the stock market is undergoing adjustments. Why not have a look first?"

Sister Feng heard this and sat down again. Tan Chun smiled and said, "Now Sister Feng wants to choose the timing again? I tell you this, whether it's for your retirement or your children's education, the best time for investment is right now! You are always hoping to enter the market when it is at the lowest. Don't let a golden opportunity slip away."

Sister Feng's face reddened and she said, "I was only thinking of buying after a short period of time. A few days do not matter."

Tan Chun solemnly replied, "Investing at a later period will perhaps bring a very different result. Just take the example of Qiao Jie's educational expense reserve. Qiao Jie is now 10 years old. Eight years from now, if she wants to go to Harvard, I estimate the expenses to be about $1.8 million. If you, from this day onward, invest $13,212 per month, according to the 1998–2005 stock fund average annual return ratio, eight years later, you can accumulate $1.8 million; but if you had immediately started investing monthly after Qiao Jie was born, with the same annual return ratio, you would only have had needed to invest a monthly sum of $3,566. Wouldn't it have been so much easier on you?"

Sister Feng was very surprised and asked, "Why is there such a huge difference with a mere eight-year delay?"

Tan Chun replied, "This is due to the effect of compound interest. The initial investment profits will also help to make money later."

Sister Feng nodded and said, "Yes, this is the meaning of interest on interest."

Bao Yu also hurriedly added, "Only Third Sister knows best. I'm forever muddle-headed, always thinking of entering the market at a low point, forgetting that the purpose of investment is to earn profits, and the advantage lies with those who start early."

At that point Grandmother Jia said, "All right! All right! I am dreadfully bored. Third Sister just came back and all of you badger her to no end. Let her rest. There are still many days ahead. What is the hurry?" After hearing this, everyone parted ways.

If you want to know what happened next, you will have to read the next chapter.

HSBC Jintrust investment advisors recommend:

The earlier you invest, the more profits you will make

You must act quickly to make profits from your investments. This is akin to two people participating in a walkathon. The earlier you set off, the more likely you can walk at a leisurely pace. Those who set off late will have to work hard to catch up. This is the benefit of early investment.

Mr. Chen started to invest $500 monthly in regular fixed-quantity funds when he was 20 years old. Suppose the average yearly return rate was 10 percent. He invested for seven years, never cutting his payment, and then stopped making payments. After that, he allowed capital grow with the profits. By the time he reached the age of retirement at 60 years old, the total investment would have reached $1.38 million. Mr. Wong, on the other hand, only started investing at the age of 27 years, investing a similar $500 per month with 10 percent average yearly return rate. He invested regularly for 33 years, never failing to make a monthly payment, and only accumulated $1.39 million at the age of 60! In comparison, Mr. Chen would have led a far more comfortable life than Mr. Wong.

Table 15.1   investment returns

	Mr. Chen	Mr. Wong
Starting age	20 years old	27 years old
Monthly investment	$500	$500
Investment period	7 years	33 years
Total repayment at age 60	$1,381,597	$1,393,577

Table 15.1 shows the overall return from two kinds of investments with different starting times and durations (assuming a 10 percent average annual return rate with monthly compound interest).

Chapter 16

Bao Yu Tells Tan Chun of Failure

Tan Chun Explains Combination to Bao Yu

I t was said that Tan Chun returned to Qiu Shuang Zhai, and for many days was busy with cleaning up her room, arranging appliances, and opening up the packages that she had brought back from America. After organizing the items according to whom they were meant for, Tan Chun asked her maid Cui Mo to distribute the perfume, handbags, cosmetics, and lipstick to Bao Chai, Dai Yu, and others.

Bao Yu lifted the curtains and entered the room. He smiled and asked, "Has Sister recovered from her jet lag yet?"

Tan Chun hurriedly rose and replied, smiling, "I am well now. Many thanks to Brother who is always thinking of me." As she spoke, she got up and ordered her servant to bring in the tea.

Tan Chun smiled and said, "It has been a few years since we last met, and you have not changed a bit, still idle..." Halfway through her sentence, she swallowed hard, pursed her lips, and smiled.

Bao Yu said, "What, 'still idling away' you wanted to say? That was my life years ago. Ever since you left for abroad, I have also started to grasp some principles!"

Tan Chun asked curiously, "Grasp what principles?"

Bao Yu smiled and replied, "Principles of managing finances, of course! Before you left to go abroad, didn't you mention that you would help me come up with a financial management plan? I couldn't wait for you to return, so I started my own investments some years ago!"

Tan Chun nodded and said, "Seems like you do realize the rationale behind investing early after all, but just how did you invest your money?"

Bao Yu proudly explained, "Didn't you mention some time back that for different stages in life, we must have different investment portfolios? I realized this even before you said it! I thought that since I'm still young, I have a better ability to withstand risks. Moreover, my investment horizon is still a long way ahead. Hence, I invested a large portion of my money in stocks."

Tan Chun smiled and said, "This is correct. So what was the outcome?" Bao Yu heard this and lowered his head in a discouraged manner. "It did not once occur to me that the stocks I bought would rise and fall collectively, and I couldn't have timed it worse. Just when I was cash-strapped, Sister Lin needed money for publishing her poetry, so I could only grit my teeth and lend it to her."

Tan Chun said, "Your problem is the irrational combination of your investment portfolio. Firstly, you did not take into consideration the liquidity of your investments. You should have bought some money market funds. The liquidity of money market funds makes them an effective cash management tool. Money market funds should be a permanent part of your investment portfolio to provide adequate liquidity throughout your lifetime."

Bao Yu replied, "This had not occurred to me, indeed. What else should I know?"

Tan Chun replied, "Secondly, you should not think that because your risk-bearing capacity is higher, you can ignore low-risk types of investments. The fact is, even young people's portfolios should also have fixed-income products; the older generation could also have stocks in their portfolios, but their portfolios have different overall risk characteristics." After hearing this, Bao Yu nodded his head repeatedly.

Tan Chun said, "Building an investment portfolio should follow the 'pyramid structure,' gradually from top to bottom. Firstly, you must pay attention to your own investment goals and risk-bearing capacity to determine your portfolio's property disposition proportion. For example, in the portfolio, 70 percent should be stocks and 30 percent fixed earning tools. Then for every category of property, it will undergo further divisions. For example, you can use 20 percent of the stock allocation to buy blue chip stocks, 10 percent on small cap, and 40 percent on stock funds. For the 30 percent of fixed earning tools, you can use 10 percent to invest in bond funds, 10 percent to invest in a money market fund, and deposit another 10 percent in the bank. The last step is to choose the best from the different types of investments, single stocks or funds with good reputations. The different categories of investment types taken together become a single combination. Management is not solely about separating your risk and lowering the vulnerability of stock fluctuation. The most important thing is the ability to optimize the portfolio's risk characteristics to help you achieve your investment target."

Bao Yu heard this and said, "You've said it right! The stocks that I bought were then the very popular technology stocks, and the risk was indeed too high." As Bao Yu finished speaking, Dai Yu strolled into the room.

If you want to know what happened next, you will have to read the next chapter.

HSBC Jintrust investment advisors recommend:

Build your portfolio from the top down, according to the "pyramid structure"

For different types of investments, profitability, security, and liquidity are different. Through establishing an investment portfolio, you will be able to complement your investments and reduce overall risk. Before an investment portfolio is established, you must first be clear about your investment horizon and your risk tolerance. For example, if your investment period is five years, and you have a higher tolerance for risk, you can be an aggressive investor. The proportion of the high-risk stocks or stock funds in your investment portfolio can be higher. At the same time, the proportion of lower risk bonds or bond funds can be reduced. After your investment portfolio's proportions have been decided upon, the next step, moving down the pyramid, would be to choose the type of investment, and to pick relatively trustworthy single stocks or funds with good past performance.

One thing to note is if your present financial managing method and the new target investment portfolio are substantially different, it is better not to adjust to the new investment portfolio all at once. If you did, you would be buying and selling large amounts during the same period. If you were down on your luck, you might also suffer a considerable loss. Consider entering the market in several separate steps. Use one or two years to finish constructing your investment portfolio. This will reduce the risk of purchasing all your funds when the market is at its peak.

Chapter 17

Comparing Clothes, Dai Yu Talks Fashion

*Explaining Trends, Tan Chun Tells
of Investment Failures*

It was said that Bao Yu was chatting with Tan Chun when the pageboy on the verandah exclaimed, "Lady Dai Yu is here!" Dai Yu walked into the room and saw that Bao Yu was also present, she smiled and said, "It is evident that your siblings have left the rest of us to come out here to chat privately. May I intrude?"

Tan Chun smiled and said, "We've not seen each other for so many years, Sister. Your words are as sharp as ever."

Dai Yu said, "I came with the original intention to thank you. You took the trouble to bring so many things, yet you left none for yourself and gave everything to us."

Tan Chun replied, "They are worth very little!"

Bao Yu noticed that Dai Yu looked tired and asked her, "Sister, aren't you supposed to be busy working on your second book of poetry these days? So what are you doing here?"

Dai Yu sighed and said, "Well, I've been thinking, readers are always chasing the latest craze. My first published book of poetry sold many copies, but that was only due to the popularity of Liu Wu Xing's 'Secret of Dream of Red Chamber Unveiled,' which created hype for all things related to 'Dream of Red Chamber.' I was lucky enough to ride the wave. Now that the hype is subsiding, everyone will be turning to the 'next big thing' on the literary scene. I don't even know how many copies of my second book I would be able to sell, so why am I even wasting my time?"

Bao Yu heard this and his mind wandered back to the network technology stocks that he was discussing with Tan Chun earlier. He said to Tan Chun in an excited voice, "That's right! It's the same with the stock market. One minute, it's all the rage, and the next, it's out moded. Network technology stocks were still 'hot' when I first bought them. Literally, the entire nation was feverish! But as it turned out, the 'net' was a self-restricting one, and now I can't even bear its slightest mention. Right now, it's also the same case with colored metal stocks. Just a while back, they were the darlings of the stock market, with leading stocks returning fivefold and up. But now, they've suddenly cooled so much that no one is even asking about them anymore."

Tan Chun smiled and said, "Demand for these stocks spread like wild fire because of two psychological phenomena. The first of these is the 'follow the crowd' mentality. Have you noticed that the phrase written in Chinese consists of four smaller 'man' characters supporting one on top? The four smaller characters are akin to the broad community of investors, while the one on top is responsible for creating the 'hot spot.' The blind following can be attributed to the 'herding effect.' The higher the stock rises, the more actively the experts recommend the stock. Secondly, people are profit-driven. Everyone sees certain stocks as flavors of the month and easy money. Hence, they are willing to expose themselves to very high risks and end up getting their fingers burnt."

Dai Yu asked, "Is following the crowd really that bad?"

Tan Chun replied, "Not necessarily. Investing by following the crowd certainly might not lead to a loss, but blindly following trends will cause one to lose one's direction and forget about the true value of investment variety, and thus, become a victim of the person who created the frenzy in the first place."

Tan Chun suddenly paused and looked Dai Yu up and down. Dai Yu asked with confusion, "What's with you, Tan Chun? You're making me very uncomfortable."

Tan Chun smiled and said, "Your outfit was made before I left for abroad." Dai Yu said proudly, "But of course. I cut it out from the cloth Sister Feng gave me for my birthday that year. Everybody was saying that the outfit's design was classic yet stylish, and could be worn for a long time. I can't be compared to those affluent ladies, who can update their wardrobes as and when they like. We are merely living under somebody else's roof. Furthermore, fashion trends are constantly changing. Following trends is easier said than done. I'm better off 'remaining steadfast in the face of changes.'"

Bao Yu smiled and said, "Tan Chun was merely making an offhand remark and yet you answered her with a barrage of words."

Tan Chun replied, "Dai Yu has put it very aptly. Investment and fashion are very similar. The market is very 'temperamental,' and is constantly changing. If you were to follow the trends, you'd spend a lot time and energy tracking stock movements, and you might still end up picking the wrong stocks to follow. Select the best stocks and hold on to them in the long run, not changing your original investment plans with every fluctuation in the market. That is the simplest and yet the most effective way to invest."

Dai Yu heard this and smiled, and nudged Bao Yu gently on his forehead. "Now do you understand? Next time, don't do anything rash when you hear about the latest trends in the market." Bao Yu rubbed his forehead and smiled with embarrassment.

If you want to know what happened next, you'll have to read the next chapter.

HSBC Jintrust investment advisors recommend:

Do not try to time the market or follow trends

You will realize along the way that as you invest, it is not always easy to maintain a long-term investment plan. This problem stems from two major emotions: fear and greed. When the market falls, the fear of losing money will cause you to change your long-term investment plans. Similarly, when the market rises and almost everyone becomes richer overnight, greed may compel you to attempt to earn more income by undertaking higher risks. "Chasing highs and killing lows" has become the biggest weakness of man, which only a select few can overcome. Therefore, even though many people think they can get their timing right, believing that they can buy at the lowest rate and sell at the highest point, the opposite is often true.

Buying low and selling high is not easy at all. Holding the stock for the long term is the easiest, yet most effective investment strategy. For example, suppose from year 1991 to year 2005, you invested in stock A at the beginning of the year during any of the 15 years and maintained the investment for one year. According to the Shanghai Composite Index return ratio computation, the probability of a negative yield is 47 percent. If you maintain the investment for three years, the probability would be 38 percent. If you maintain it for six years, the probability would be 10 percent. However, if you maintain it for a full nine years, the probability of a negative yield would drop to zero. At least this would ensure that you would not lose any money!

Chapter 18

Sister Feng Repeats Her Mistakes Due to Greed

Bao Yu is Admired for His Character

When Bao Yu and Dai Yu were both in the room chatting with Tan Chun, they heard someone call from the outside, "Second Mistress arrives!" They all knew that Sister Feng had come, and hurriedly rose to greet her.

Sister Feng entered with a piece of paper in her hand. She smiled and said, "You two are even earlier than I am. Are you here to consult the finance management guru?"

Tan Chun said, "Sister Feng, you're the real guru within the business circle, so don't tease me!"

Sister Feng replied, "Knowing how to do business does not mean you know how to manage your finances. Everyone has his or her own niche."

Tan Chun said, "Even so, how could I be compared to you?"

Sister Feng replied, "What nonsense! I have come here to ask for your opinion. Some time ago, you recommended regular fixed-quantity investment funds, right? I also feel that this is the easiest and most efficient method to invest, most suited for a busy woman like me. I went to the bank yesterday to buy this fund. But as luck would have it, someone from a nearby counter told me that the net value of the fund that I was originally planning to buy had recently risen very quickly, so, instead of buying something that has become more expensive, why not go for funds for which the net value is below the face value? I thought it over and felt that that was true. I spend $50,000 and I buy funds worth $2 per share. If you don't take cost into consideration, my share in my original fund would only be 25,000 shares. But if I buy a $0.90 fund, I can actually get more than 55,000 shares. Isn't this much cheaper?" As she said this, she passed the piece of paper she was holding to Tan Chun and continued, "This is the brochure for the fund that I bought. Can you help me understand if this investment is appropriate?"

Tan Chun took the paper and Bao Yu sat beside Tan Chun so they could pore over it together.

Tan Chun read it without saying a single word. Sister Feng became anxious and asked, "How is it?"

Tan Chun forced a smile and said, "Sister Feng, it looks like you took the wrong advice again. This fund's past results have always been wavering back and forth below face value. The fund manager's managing capacity is very dubious."

Sister Feng heard this and regretted her actions deeply. She felt embarrassed and angry, and lowered her head without a word.

Bao Yu said hurriedly, "Sister Feng, you don't have to take this to heart. Everyone makes mistakes. Before you came in,

Tan Chun was also reprimanding me for buying stocks solely by following trends."

Tan Chun added, "Everyone thinks that they are rational beings, but in truth, everyone's rationality is limited. When people are making decisions, it is hard to calculate a product's true worth. You only use the easier clues to make your decision. Look at Bao Yu, he has bought stocks based on their popularity. Sister Feng, you rely on prices to decide which fund to buy. The fact is, these criteria will not bring us any profit."

Tan Chun saw Dai Yu flipping through the books that she had brought back from America, and said to her, "You've grown to become a beautiful and famous author these few years. The number of suitors must have trampled our door flat. But why are you still set only on Bao Yu?"

Dai Yu heard this and blushed fiercely and scolded Tan Chun: "This girl must have lost her mind! Fancy you saying such improper things!"

Sister Feng smiled and said, "Trust Tan Chun to be so frank! But why don't you tell us? We are all so curious!"

Dai Yu smiled shyly and said, "Those suitors were all rich and powerful, but how can that compare to what Bao Yu and I shared throughout our childhood? We have a perfect understanding of each other. Furthermore, all the wealth and fame don't matter much to me. Even though Bao Yu has not achieved much yet, what impresses me most is his good character and his loyalty toward me. Do you still remember the time Zi Juan was only joking with him about us returning to the South and he ended up being sick for days?"

Tan Chun nodded and said, "What Dai Yu just said is also applicable to investment. Investing is similar to choosing a lifelong partner; the most important things to consider are the investment type and its intrinsic value."

If you want to know what happened next, you'll have to read the next chapter.

HSBC Jintrust investment advisors recommend:

Focus on the intrinsic value of your investment type

Consider two open-ended funds, one which is a new fund with a face value of $1, the other one an old fund with a net worth of $1.20. Investors like to buy the new fund, as it seems cheaper. But in actual fact, open-ended funds are not divided into cheap or expensive ones. The fund's current net worth will not decide your future investment return. As an investor, you must not solely take into consideration the net worth of the fund when choosing between the old and the new fund. The most important thing is to look at the fund's intrinsic value. This includes the fund manager's management ability, the team's professionalism, as well as past performance and growth potential.

The truth is, the old fund's performance has withstood various tests of the market. The investors can make quite an objective judgment of the fund manager's ability by inspecting the fund's past income and risk. Moreover, high net worth old funds could be a sign of the fund manager's outstanding ability. Investors' preference for new over old could be the reason that many lose profit opportunities in the long run.

Chapter 19

The Foolish in Love Throws Away All Reason

Tan Chun Uses Jade to Explain Value Investment

I t was said that Tan Chun was telling Sister Feng about the need to pay attention to the intrinsic value of investment variety. She said, "Take, for example, buying stocks. Choosing good companies is more pertinent than choosing stocks that are cheap. Even though good company stocks do not come cheap, as long as the price is reasonable, they are still worthwhile to buy."

Bao Yu said, "Tan Chun, what you mean by a truly 'good company' is not simply what normal investors would assume by just consulting newspapers or magazines, right?"

Tan Chun nodded and said, "Precisely. A so-called 'good company' is only identified after careful analysis, and it conforms to the principles of a 'value investment.'"

Sister Feng asked curiously, "What is a value investment?"

As Sister Feng spoke, a servant entered the room and said, "Master, please come outside and take a look. Bei Ming is at the door saying he has some urgent business with you."

Bao Yu hurriedly said, "I'll be right back," and left the room, leaving Tan Chun, Dai Yu, and Sister Feng to gossip freely. Dai Yu could not stop worrying about Bao Yu, so she gave half-hearted responses to the girls' chitchat.

After a short while, Bao Yu returned with a downcast look. Dai Yu immediately asked Bao Yu what was wrong, but Bao Yu refused to answer her. Dai Yu got impatient and stamped her foot: "Just say it, be it good or bad. Keeping quiet makes us all the more worried!"

Bao Yu said, "Fine! Then I'll tell it straight! Didn't you want to publish a second book of poetry? Well, I knew you needed money back then, so I thought of pawning my jade to get money." Dai Yu heard this and didn't know whether to be happy or shocked. She was happy over the fact that she made the right choice in Bao Yu, for he genuinely cared for her. The shock came from knowing that Bao Yu's jade was a priceless gem of the entire Jia family, and if word of this were to spread, the entire household would be in upheaval.

Tears rolled down her face and she sobbed. "Why did you bother to do this?"

Bao Yu smiled and said, "I've never cherished that nuisance right from the start; selling it off wouldn't bother me. It was a pity I let Bei Ming take the jade to the pawnshop, though. That ignorant fool of a pawnshop owner, who did not know how to judge quality, said that the quality and color were just average, not worth several thousand."

Sister Feng said, "Brother Bao, please don't do anything foolish anymore. How could your precious jade be compared to any other common jade? You were brought into this world together with this jade. It can ward off evil spirits, dissolve all calamities into blessings, and its divine powers are most definitely effective!"

Tan Chun also added, "I think it is really improper of Bao Yu to sell his jade. If our mother hears about it, we won't have a single day of peace around here. If she asks you why you wanted to sell your jade in the first place, won't this implicate Dai Yu as well?"

Bao Yu heard this and felt that it made a lot of sense, so he said in the end, "Fine then, we'll just have to think of other ways."

Tan Chun smiled and said, "So Bao Yu's magical jade in actual fact is not worth much, and back home, we all viewed it as a piece of treasure. To really know how much something is worth, you have to use fundamental facts and effective tools to appraise its value. It is the same principle as the value investment Sister Feng asked about."

Sister Feng smiled and said, "Tan Chun, you are talking about investments again!"

Tan Chun said, "Value investment has to do with the estimated value. When the investor is analyzing the company, he should picture himself as the company's sole owner, carefully analyze the company's overall management quality and the trustworthiness of the management, as well as the company's competitive advantage and whether it is sustainable, and so on. Then use some models and benchmarks to estimate the intrinsic value of the shares. Those companies with intrinsic values that are higher than market prices are the 'good companies' that are worth investing in."

Sister Feng frowned and said, "How would the ordinary investor know how to estimate value?"

Tan Chun replied, "If your ability to estimate is limited, there are two solutions. The first is to avoid unfamiliar domains and invest strictly within your own area of competence. The second is to engage a professional to estimate the value on your behalf. For instance, seek advice from consultants, or buy investments that do not need much value estimation ability, such as index funds."

While Tan Chun was explaining, a servant entered and said, "First Mistress invites Tan Chun and Bao Yu over." Sister Feng and Dai Yu took their leave and Tan Chun and Bao Yu followed the servant over to Lady Wang's side.

If you want to know what happened next, you'll have to read the following chapter.

HSBC Jintrust investment advisors recommend:

Value investment's basic principle is to buy a good company with a price that is lower than its value

Even though the value of everything in this world is rather subjective, and can differ from person to person, there is still a common basis upon which the value of most items can be assessed. For an enterprise, there is already a value appraisal method that is generally accepted by most people: its value is equivalent to the sum of the current value of all its cash flows. As for the actual estimation of value, it would depend on the strengths of each individual investor. If an investor is unable to reasonably estimate a company's intrinsic value, he or she should not buy that company's stock, for this person is simply not capable of making that investment decision alone.

Chapter 20

Lady Wang Buys Insurance with a Muddled Head

*Jia Bao Yu Understands and Makes an
Alternate Proposal*

Tan Chun and Bao Yu followed the servant in from the garden. They entered the room only to see Lady Wang sitting inside shedding tears. When she saw that they had arrived, Lady Wang cried out, "My children, here you are! Tan Chun, quickly help me think of a solution. My $100,000 of retirement money will soon be gone!"

Tan Chun and Bao Yu immediately asked her why that should be. Lady Wang said tearfully, "I am 50 years old already, and I will soon be retiring. Two years ago, your Aunt Xue told me that nowadays, the social pension scheme is definitely inadequate to cover expenses for food and clothes after retirement. I can only rely on myself after retirement. Hence, I purchased four bonus insurance policies jointly with her. I was hoping originally that the yearly payment would exceed the interest I could get in a bank. I did not expect that last year's dividend would amount to zero. I calculated the yearly return ratio and it was even lower than 0.5 percent. Earlier today, I thought of canceling one of the policies. Only when I asked your Aunt Xue did I find out that an administrative fee is charged for terminating a policy. At this rate, what's left of my $100,000 premiums will be less than $80,000! Initially, I thought that buying insurance could 'insure' me. I don't want to be making less than deposit income, and I'm worried about the possibility of my property shrinking. What should I do?"

As she said this, she handed a piece of paper to Tan Chun and said, "When the insurance agent was recommending various policy types, he handed me this 'benefit illustration' table. On it, it clearly stated that the 'projected minimum dividend' for the first year should be almost $1,000, but why is the actual bonus received only $500, which is half the 'projected minimum dividend'? Is what he said not reliable?"

Tan Chun took the piece of paper and read it through and smiled. "Do you know where bonus insurance's dividends come from? They come from 'interest difference' and 'mortality difference.' The former refers to the difference between the actual investment rate of return (IRR) and the projected IRR. The latter refers to the difference between the actual mortality rate and the projected mortality rate. The sum of 'interest difference' and 'mortality difference' is the source of life insurance companies' main earnings. Different insurance companies also have different methods of assigning earnings. For example, policyholders may get 70 percent and the insurance company 30 percent. This means that for every $10, policyholders receive $7 and the insurance company receives $3. Since dividends are influenced by the insurance company's investment level, calculations, and various other factors, just how much dividend money there is to be divided is uncertain. The bonus illustration shown in brochures cannot be taken as future anticipated actual returns, but can only be taken as a reference. Did the agent state that clearly to you?"

Lady Wang thought for a while and said, "I think there was some mention of 'the insurance company would not be able to guarantee the amount of dividend' or something along that line. I don't remember anymore."

Tan Chun said, "You don't have to rush into terminating your policy just because the first-year dividend was low. Firstly, terminating your policy will cause you to incur many types of charges. It is not worth it at all. Secondly, you need not be overly concerned about initial returns. Bonus insurance works pretty much the same way as investment-linked insurance for which, during good market performance, the returns can be considerably higher. It is better to look at the long-term income."

Lady Wang heard this and was somewhat relieved. She sighed. "But it seems that the insured income might not necessarily be able to defend against inflation."

Bao Yu clapped and said, "Mother finally understands! In the earlier years, the Insurance Regulatory Commission had a top limit of 2.5 percent for long-term insurance products' return ratio, causing the return ratios of retirement insurance products to have an average value of only 2.3 percent. This is hardly enough protection against inflation rates for the next 10 to 20 years or more. Now that life insurance companies have made improvements to the retiree insurance product, with the inclusion of bonus, multi-purpose, or more complicated insurance schemes, they have transformed the fixed rate into a floating rate. This change will enhance retiree insurance products' inflation resistance ability. However, an insurance product should be focused on its core purpose of providing financial safeguards. Talking about resisting inflation, insurance may not be able to be compared to other types of investments. Let's talk about funds; projected returns are directly related to actual investment returns, but operation costs are much lower than those for the insurance company. Theoretically, its inflation resistance ability is stronger."

When she finished speaking, Bao Yu smiled and nestled himself into Lady Wang's arms, saying, "Let me recommend for you the best retirement finance management plan. It would be social pension plus funds plus me! If you let me manage your funds, you will do even better!"

Lady Wang stroked Bao Yu's head and said, "As the saying goes, raise children to provide for old age. I only have you. If I don't depend on you, who else can I depend upon?"

If you want to know what happened next, you will have to read the next chapter.

HSBC Jintrust investment advisors recommend:

The basis of insurance finance management is safeguarding life and health

When you buy insurance, you must always return to its fundamental purpose, which is to provide a safeguard. The insurance plan should start with accident and health insurance. With accident insurance, the insured can obtain compensation after any mishap. On the other hand, health insurance safeguards your funds if you fall ill and require a hospital stay. If you do not have these basic safeguards and yet are considering other insurance types, it would be as inappropriate as talking to a malnourished person about nutrition. You should observe the following sequence when you buy insurance: accident (life insurance) → health insurance (including major illnesses, medical insurance) → education insurance → retirement insurance → bonus insurance, dividends and multi-purpose insurance. In the process of buying insurance, you must bear in mind the "double 10 rule"; that is, to be wary that "the insurance amount must not exceed 10 times the household's income," and "the family's yearly total insurance premiums should not exceed 10 percent of the family's yearly income."

Chapter 21

Disagreement Occurs During Shi Xiang Yun's Honeymoon

Tan Chun Teases the New Bride

Bao Yu was recommending to Lady Wang a scheme to manage wealth that was meant to let her enjoy her old age.

"Just depending on the social security system will not be enough. You should invest in some products that can resist inflation, such as funds or bonds; if those are of no use, there's still me. Mother, you gave me my life. If I did not repay you, wouldn't that mean you doted on me for nothing?"

Lady Wang was happy hearing this, and even Tan Chun went on to comment in jest, "Second Brother so rarely shows his family dedication! With this little display of his, who can resent our Grand Mistress and Second Mistress for doting on him so much?"

Lady Wang became even more elated, and instructed her servants to take some of her playthings and give them to Bao Yu. After another round of laughter, Bao Yu and Tan Chun went their own ways.

Just when Tan Chun had returned to her room with the intention to rest a bit, she heard her servants reporting, "Miss Shi has come."

Tan Chun was just about to invite Xiang Yun in, but she had already entered. Tan Chun grinned. "I heard that you have married."

Xiang Yun blushed and bowed her head, concentrating on her tea.

Tan Chun asked, "Wasn't it icing on the cake? I heard that your husband is dashing, and has an even disposition. His talent and aptitude in literature and art are not beneath Second Brother's!"

Unexpectedly, upon hearing these words, Xiang Yun's face turned solemn, and she said angrily, "We quarreled a few times during the honeymoon. Now I regret choosing the wrong person to marry!"

Tan Chun asked nervously, "What do you mean?"

Xiang Yun replied sadly, "While on honeymoon in the Maldives, I found out that he doesn't know how to manage money at all. He has many bankcards, a bank account for his pay, and another one for his car installments. He even had another account for buying the plane tickets for our honeymoon. I have been thrown into confusion by his pile of bankcards. To think that he's the Finance Director in his company! He is but a paper tiger!"

Tan Chun smiled and asked, "And how about you?"

Xiang Yun's face turned red and she said, "He saw my credit card bill, and said that I spend too extravagantly, that I have no control. But what bride would not try her best to prepare for her wedding? Why did he have to make a mountain out of a molehill? In the Maldives, whenever I proposed where we should eat or go for entertainment, he'd say that one's too expensive, and that one's not worth the price. It was such a damper."

Tan Chun nodded, agreeing. "Right. A research study in America has shown that finances are one of the main reasons newly married couples argue. You have to be careful; quarreling over money problems has a more serious impact than most other arguments."

Xiang Yun furrowed her brow. "Then what should I do?"

Tan Chun said, "First, both you and your husband will have to adjust your way of thinking. From now on, it is different from the past when you both did not have a care in the world. It used to be that each of your incomes and expenditures and even liabilities belonged to just you. But after marriage, both of you have to share the burden. You two have to have in your hearts the concept of 'us,' making actions based on the overall picture, not just being concerned about your own wants."

"I think both of us are able to do that. What else?"

"Secondly, it's a marriage of persons, a union of finances. The Americans have done research that shows that couples who independently maintain their own assets are more likely to divorce than those who share property. Prior to marriage, both parties may have several properties and some scattered investments, but now that two people are living together, both of you have to tidy up and merge accounts. That way, you'll be able to understand the family's overall financial situation. If you have a bank account here and another bankcard there, then in the end, nobody will know exactly how much money there is in the family. In addition, you can unify and mobilize the family's assets, and then make distributions and investments as a family.

Xiang Yun nodded profusely upon hearing Tan Chun's explanation, and then said, "This has indeed touched the bottom of my heart. I have roughly calculated both our individual investments from before we were married, and found out that we invested way too much in national debt. Are we being too conservative?"

Tan Chun replied, "Both of you are young. Of course, you have to consider taking moderate risk and raising the rate of growth of the family's assets. Don't forget that both of you have to prepare funds for raising children!"

Xiang Yun blushed, and just before she could reply, she heard the servant outside reporting, "Master Wei has come."

Tan Chun smiled. "Both of you are so in love, that Son-in-law Wei can barely leave you for a moment!" She nudged Xiang Yun forward and continued, "You'd better be quick, and save him from concern."

Xiang Yun said, "Tan is poking fun at me, but I certainly am not going to budge!"

Just then, Wei Ruo Lan walked in.

What happened next will be uncovered in the following chapter.

HSBC Jintrust investment advisors recommend:

When married, do not manage your finances separately, as if you were single

After marrying, many couples still are not able to shake off the habits they had when they were single, and only care about themselves when it comes to wealth management. However, this is not a very sensible arrangement.

If you neglect the fact that you and your partner are actually an entity—with common assets, income, pension funds, and liabilities—you will find it very hard to make reasonable and effective arrangements with regard to your joint wealth.

If a married couple still behaves the same way they did when they were single, separating everything very clearly, that is just like having a company's different departments keeping individual ledger books, concealing many troubles.

Types of trouble that may happen to a couple include two people making repetitive and unnecessary investments; or having a lot of cash on hand, instead of in investments; or making some investment decisions that lead to assets not being made use of properly.

That is why when people get married, their money must be merged, too. That means tidying up and merging the two persons' accounts; merging and mobilizing the family's assets; redistributing assignments and investments; and so on.

Chapter 22

The Intelligent Lass Clarifies Financial Responsibilities

The Newlyweds Ponder Raising Children

Xiang Yun was in Tan Chun's room talking when Wei Ruo Lan walked in. Tan Chun smiled and said, "Ruo Lan, please take your new bride home, so that this chatterbox will stop prattling here. It's so noisy that I really can't stand it anymore."

Ruo Lan had originally been worried over a tiff he had with Xiang Yun earlier that day and had come looking for her. What Tan Chun said exactly served his intentions, so he quickly pulled Xiang Yun aside and said, "Good sister, stop being a bother. It was my fault earlier; I shouldn't have reprimanded you for being a spendthrift. We should go back now, and let Third Missy rest."

Xiang Yun brushed him off. "Don't try to use honeyed words to humor me. If you don't say clearly who's in charge of managing finances in the family from now on, then I won't go back!"

Ruo Lan knew that it would be difficult to turn the tide to his favor now, and he looked at Tan Chun for help. Tan Chun smiled and said, "Listen to me, Sister Shi, you should stop being so troubled over this. Ruo Lan, you should not chide her for no reason. I have an idea. From now on, both of you can apply central management on a democratic basis. Wei is deep and thorough in planning, and should be responsible for the larger expenses like houses and cars. Yun, who is used to extravagant spending, should take care of smaller expenses such as meals, utilities, gas, and phone bills. This way, you'll be able to experience what it's like to manage a household. At the same time, you can each make monthly deposits into a shared bank account to be used for savings and investments. Any remaining money can then be spent at your own discretion. This way, both of you will be able to experience the responsibilities and obligations of your family, and still be able to preserve a little of the freedom you had when you were single. Isn't that killing two birds with one stone?"

Xiang Yun and Ruo Lan agreed that it was a good idea.

Ruo Lan saw that Xiang Yun's facial expression had turned gentler, and he asked her to sit down. He asked, beaming, "So what were you guys talking about when I entered? What was so funny?"

Xiang Yun replied hurriedly, "We weren't talking about anything."

But Tan Chun grinned and said, "We were just talking about when you'll be promoted to becoming a father."

Ruo Lan just sighed. "Now that we have to pay for our house and a car, how will we be able to afford raising a child?"

Tan Chun said, "Your worries are not unfounded. Having a child does require a lot of planning. Most people would consider having children to be an emotional decision, and neglect it being very much an economic one, too. Having a child is similar to making an investment. The only difference is that a child can bring you happiness. As they say, there is no such thing as a free lunch. To attain happiness, you naturally have to pay a price. When an enterprise invests in a new business, they have to estimate the capital needed to build and run it, and calculate how much profit it'll bring in the future. However, few couples use a similar decision strategy before having a child. Nonetheless, money will still affect the child's life in multiple ways in the future. He or she will be affected by the district that he or she is brought up in, the kindergarten that you choose, and the level of education that you can provide. If you manage to calculate as accurately as you can the capital needed to bring up a child, you will have more choices in the future, and you will more likely be able to fulfill your child's and your dreams."

Xiang Yun furrowed her brow. "I saw this in the newspaper: a sociology expert who did some research on the cost to raise a child calculated that the amount of money that is require to raise a child to 30 years old is $490,000. That was quite a shock!"

Tan Chun smiled. "That scared you? I have even scarier news. The research has not factored in inflation, and in these last few years, the inflation rate for education fees has been shocking."

Xiang Yun gulped upon hearing this. "We just bought and renovated our house, and there's not much savings left. What should we do?"

Grinning, Tan Chun said to her, "For both of you, accumulating funds for your child will just have to be part of your daily budget. Just deposit a fixed proportion of the money from your pay every month into that fund, and save through fixed deposits or regular fixed investments. When 'many a little makes a mickle,' you'll be able to save enough."

Xiang Yun nudged her laughingly. "Regular fixed deposits, again? Are you possessed or something? You're always talking about them." Tan Chun just laughed along.

Please look at the next chapter to see what happened next.

HSBC Jintrust investment advisors recommend:

Apply enterprise-like techniques when planning family finances

When handling family finances, you can apply the same concepts a company does. When every family member develops a formal, business-like perspective, the tendency to act impetuously will disappear. Then you'll be able to employ professional strategies, such as the way a company does cost estimation, predicting its future profits; how a company plans expenditures and distributes work properly, and intelligently implements goals according to their importance and urgency; how a company does regular checks on cash flow statements and balance sheets, and effectively controls the process of reaching its goal; and so on.

In truth, when two people decide to share and realize a dream, such a relationship is identical to the practices of a business venture—pooling time and effort, making use of teamwork, and reaching common goals in the allotted time. Undisputedly, a family is much like running an enterprise, but the company you are running is the enterprise of your life.

Chapter 23

Misspendings of the "Month Bare" Tribe

Tan Chun Teaches Effective Planning

Word has it that Xiang Yun and her husband had made enquiries about the accumulation of a child's funds from Tan Chun, and talked together about it before taking their leave. By then, Tan Chun was feeling tired and decided to rest.

The following morning, Tan Chun woke up to fine weather and, with no tasks at hand, loitered around the corridor, playing with the birds, before going out into the yard. She then followed the Qin Fang (or Fragrant) stream, watching the goldfish swimming in it, past Ou Xiang (or Sweet Lotus) pavilion, and through the veranda. Lifting her head and setting her eyes on the lintel, she noticed the words "Fragrant Harbor." "Isn't this Fourth Sister's bedroom? Since I'm here already, I might as well pay her a visit."

At that same moment, Ru Hua came out and said, "Third Missy, you came at an inappropriate time, as Fourth Missy has gone out to make some purchases." Tan Chun exclaimed with a little laugh, "It does not matter. I am just here for a stroll, and since I have been hearing so much praise about Fourth Sister's paintings, I wanted to have a look at the famed beauty of the pieces of art."

Ru Hua replied, "If that's the case, please follow me, Third Young Mistress." Ru Hua then invited Tan Chun into the room. Tan Chun entered to see many scrolls stacked against the wall, protected by a veil of cloth. When the draperies were removed, she was surprised to find that the scrolls all contained paintings of magnificent scenery. "I have always known that Xi Chun painted exquisite towers and buildings, but she's improved so much and now she paints scenery, too!"

Ru Hua replied, "Third Missy, this is something you might not know. Fourth Missy is always broke at the end of the month, and she does not care much about what she does. She will simply accept any job offer she gets."

"So Fourth Sister has undergone a transition from a young talented artist to a member of the 'month bare' tribe?" Tan Chun remarked in a disappointed tone. As they conversed, Xi Chun entered the room with bags in both hands.

Throwing the bags on the floor, she said, "I am so tired!"

"Sister, where have you been shopping?" asked Tan Chun.

"Third Sister, you should go out right now to shop, too! There is a promotion going on at Capital Department Store, and it's the last day! I found lots of cheap goodies there, like this Hello Kitty handbag! Isn't it adorable?" said Xi Chun in a self-satisfied tone.

Tan Chun shook her head and said, "So that is how you have become one of the 'month bare' tribe! The way you spend, your money certainly won't last you till the end of the month!" Xi Chun blushed, and urged Tan Chun, "Third Sister, quickly teach me! I've never been able to keep track of my money or understand why I run out of it at the end of every month, so I have no choice but to take on any job available!"

"To change the 'month bare' tribes' habit isn't that difficult. Most importantly, limit your budget and always buy just the items on your shopping list; don't buy on impulse. The purse that you're holding now is unnecessary, and look at how many purses you have lying around in your bedroom right now! Why not adopt a simple and effective habit of doing your own accounting? By recording your daily expenses, you can clearly differentiate between necessities and luxuries. You will also be constantly reminded of how much you have spent. Persevere for a month and the art of spending wisely will be learned. Secondly comes regular savings. You can consider a multi-step savings method. According to your circumstances, take $2,000 to $5,000 and open a three-month fixed-deposit account each month for the first three months. From the fourth month onward, you will have one account maturing every month. If the money is not withdrawn, the remaining amounts will automatically be converted into six-month, one-year, or two-year interest rates. Then, between the fourth and sixth months, continue to set aside amounts and make fixed deposits the same way for a total of six months' fixed deposits. This multi-step approach not only guarantees an account maturing every month, but it also gives you continuous growth of the total liquid amount. After completing the initial stages of accumulating funds, the final step would be investments. Given your tender age and light family burden, you might not need to insure yourself too much. But for investments, the case is different. If you put $1,000 per month into investments, the money will snowball. As time goes by, you will no longer find yourself strapped for cash at the end of every month!" explained Tan Chun.

Xi Chun nodded in agreement, and Tan Chun added, "After all that I've taught you, what should I get as a gesture of thanks? How about a portrait done by this talented female artist?"

Xi Chun blushed and asked her sister not to tease her further. "I only take up the brush for pleasure. How can I even be called an artist?"

If you want to know what happened next, you will have to read the next chapter.

HSBC Jintrust investment advisors recommend:

Nurture the habit of accounting

Some people have said that accounting is like a lady applying her lipstick every day. To men, accounting may be likened to polishing shoes every day before stepping out of the house. Be it applying lipstick or polishing shoes, habitual accounting is recommended for everyone, and will help transform the lifestyles of those of the "month bare" tribe. There are many methods of accounting. One of them is using a small notebook to keep track of one's expenses. Using Microsoft Excel spreadsheets to record daily expenses is also useful. The Internet has several free-to-use home financing software packages, with user-friendly interfaces and comprehensive functionality that cover all potential types of revenue and expenses. However, it is important to remember that accounting is only the method, and not the goal. The true goal of using such methods is to adjust and control one's expenses.

Chapter 24

Through Many Trials and Tribulations, Xiang Mai Supports the Family

Xue Pan Turns Over a New Leaf and Becomes an Entrepreneur

I t was said that Tan Chun asked Xi Chun to do a painting for her. Xi Chun couldn't come up with any excuses, and so had to agree. Tan Chun then thanked her before taking her leave.

In the blink of an eye, it was nearing the end of the 12th month. Everyone in the Rong and Ning Mansions was busy buying New Year goodies and cleaning rooms, and everywhere was abuzz with activities. One morning, after Tan Chun got up from bed, and washed and combed her hair, she stood idly in the garden watching the maids put up spring couplets. At this moment, Xue Pan brought Xiang Mai in. Tan Chun hurriedly said, "I just heard the news about you, Brother Xue, and I was going to come and congratulate you. I didn't expect both of you to be here already!"

Xue Pan's face reddened and he said, "It is not worth congratulations. I was just released from jail." He nudged Xiang Mai forward and smilingly said, "Let me proudly introduce to you the Xue family's new daughter-in-law, Xiang Mai!"

Tan Chun nodded and said, "This is the way it should be. Xiang Mai has endured so much hardship with you all these years." As she said so, she took Xiang Mai's hand and said, "First Mistress Xue, please enter!"

Xiang Mai blushed furiously and said, "Tan Chun, don't be like this. I don't want to be made fun of!"

The trio entered the room joking and laughing happily. They sat down and started catching up. Tan Chun asked, "Xue Pan, what are your plans from now on?"

Xue Pan replied solemnly, "I've learnt from my mistakes, and from now on, I swear not to make those mistakes again. After I was convicted, my pawnshop business went on a steep decline. I have been contemplating closing the shop down, selling it, and using that money to start a new business. I might even turn into a millionaire overnight!"

Tan Chun frowned and said, "I don't mean to be a wet blanket. I know that you've always been a businessman, but you've never once held an abacus, right?"

Xue Pan rubbed his head and said, "This is exactly what I wanted to say! This is why I've come here today to discuss certain things with you."

Tan Chun pondered for a moment and said, "It is extremely important that an entrepreneur know how to manage his finances, but most people don't seem to comprehend this. In their point of view, the most important task for an entrepreneur is to find a good project. But they neglect the project's fund-managing activities. The fact is that if there's no accumulation of start-up funds for the project, or skillful utilization of funds during the project's process, or a reasonable distribution of funds, it won't succeed even if you manage to find a really good project. Some people have analyzed the successful entrepreneurs' experiences and found a common factor—that they are good at managing their finances. Therefore, even if they were unsure of the project that they had chosen, they were never unsure of the amount of funds that they had on hand. That is why, Brother Pan, if you want to be an entrepreneur, you must first think about whether you have adequate financial management ability."

Xue Pan replied, "It does not matter. In any case, I still have Xiang Mai. During those years I was in jail, Xiang Mai had to manage the family all on her own. She is so much more experienced and well informed now!"

Xiang Mai waved this compliment away and said, "That was my duty. You don't have to mention it. But regarding this entrepreneurship matter, I don't think you should dream about being a millionaire overnight. It's such words that bring out the gambler in you. You have no regard at all for the aftermath."

Xue Pan nodded and said, "I need you to keep me in check."

Tan Chun smiled and said, "With Xiang Mai helping you to manage things, I don't see a need to be worried anymore. But there's one more thing you should take note of. As the saying goes, 'never put all your eggs in one basket.' This financial management principle has never once failed and has withstood the test of time. It is no exception when you choose your business investment project. You must choose your project wisely and the funds must not be too centralized, so that when you encounter any difficulties, you can adjust swiftly, and lower the risks."

Xue Pan said, "I understand this concept. It's the same as when I go fishing. I put the fish bait on several different fishing rods. That way, even if one bait is not eaten, the other bait might have better luck, and I won't have to go home empty handed."

Tan Chun smiled and said, "This is surprising. Have you taken a liking to such leisurely activities as well?"

Xue Pan replied, "I will never go to the rowdy places of the past again." After chatting for a while more, Xue Pan and Xiang Mai bade their farewells.

If you want to know what happened next, you will have to read the next chapter.

HSBC Jintrust investment advisors recommend:

Moderate dispersion is the best form of investment protection

Suppose we were to divide a sum of money into five equal portions, to be used respectively for investment in products A, B, C, D, and E. Distribution of the investments is as shown in table 24.1.

Table 24.1   Investment distribution

Investment Product A	Investment Product B	Investment Product C	Investment Product D	Investment Product E
5,000	5,000	5,000	5,000	5,000

The annual return rates of these investment products for the next 20 years would be as shown in table 24.2.

Table 24.2   Investment returns

Investment Product A	Investment Product B	Investment Product C	Investment Product D	Investment Product E
Yearly +15%	Yearly +5%	Yearly +0%	Yearly −5%	Yearly −15%

What do you think your returns would be if you held these investment products for 20 years? By merely looking at the return rates illustrated above, many investors would probably assume the total profits after 20 years to be zero. That is, the total investment would be worth $25,000. It may surprise you that calculations based on the above rates show that your total return after 20 years is really $102,085. This amount is equivalent to more than four times the original invested sum, providing an annual return rate of 7.29 percent!

This example shows the importance of compounding interest and diversifying investments. Judging from nominal rates of return of the individual investment products, you might deem this to be a horrible total portfolio combination—of the five investments, two brought continuous losses. Product C contributed nothing, Product B performed under expectations. Only Product A performed well with an annual return rate of 15 percent. However, it is portfolio combinations like these that allow an annual rate of return (ROR) of 7.3 percent. In other words, when you diversify your investments, it is sufficient to have just a portion performing well; not all of your investments need to achieve fantastic return rates.

Chapter 25

Doting Grandmother Worries About Grandson

Tan Chun Introduces Trust

I n a blink of an eye, it was already Lunar New Year's eve. The Ning and Rong Houses were decorated for the festivities. Feasts were thrown in the halls and backyards. There was continuous chattering, laughing, and firecrackers going off. Grandmother Jia had given orders to hold a feast for several tables in the Hall. She called for a group of mini-opera performers and invited the second and third generations of the Ning and Rong houses to turn up for the family banquet.

Tan Chun arrived early. Upon seeing that Grandmother Jia was playing mahjong with Aunt Xue and Sister Feng, she thought she would take a stroll along the corridors to admire the lights put up for the festivities, and come back later.

Just as she was about to turn around, Grandmother Jia caught sight of her and cried out, "My dear, why don't you come in, since you're already here?"

Tan Chun hurried in to pay her respects. "Tan Chun is intelligent. Sit next to me and assist me," said Grandmother Jia. Tan Chun agreed.

Sister Feng sighed as Tan Chun took her seat. "This will make our old ancestor even more powerful now. I'm afraid that the red packets to be given out later may very well be all won away; I'd better have Ping-er prepare more money." This got everyone laughing.

While shuffling the tiles, Tan Chun asked, "Why isn't Second Brother back yet?"

"Your Second Brother has fallen ill due to the intensive study program his father has given him," replied Grandmother Jia. "Xi Ren came to inform us that he would only be able to come later."

"Of all the sons and grandsons, Bao Yu worries me the most," she continued, and as she said that, she took a tile. "I heard that everyone has been asking you about the investment difficulties they have been facing," she said, turning to Tan Chun. "Is there any way to put my mind at ease, to know that Bao Yu will be well taken care of even as I breathe my last breath?"

Sister Feng quickly replied, "Do not worry, and just let nature take its course."

Tan Chun laughed. "Her Old Ladyship dotes on Bao Yu so much she wishes to continue taking care of him through time and space—that is not an impossible feat."

Grandmother Jia, surprised, proceeded immediately to ask, "How could that be possible?"

Tan Chun explained, "You could set aside a portion of your assets to set up a trust. Due to the unique independent nature of trust assets, there is an isolating barrier protecting the assets of the grantor and trustee." She continued, "Creditors of grantors and trustees will not be able to use the trust assets for repayment of debts. Because of this, trusts can be used as a tool for wealth inheritance. You may entrust your assets to trust companies and sign an agreement to allow Second Brother to receive a monthly sum from the trust. That will be better than if you give him the whole sum, just in case he mismanages it, lest he live up to the saying of 'prosperity not surviving past three generations!'"

Sister Feng agreed. "This doesn't seem like a bad idea. How is it that I haven't heard of it before?"

"There's a reason for this. Individual trusts are very popular in Western cultures because most of those countries impose a high inheritance tax. To avoid taxes, many prestigious families have no choice but to entrust their assets to professional trust institutions and name their children as beneficiaries," explained Tan Chun.

"However, as our country's Inheritance Tax Law has yet to be drafted, using an individual trust as an investment method is still not as popular. Then again, it is believed that if the number of people as rich as Sister Feng increases, there will be more reason for these individual trusts to develop," she continued.

"After all, individual trusts benefit from professional management and reduction of operational costs due to their collective management. In addition, they allow the grantor to customize the trust to meet his or her needs, within the constraints of the law, achieving purposes such as managing assets, avoiding disputes over inheritance, guardianship of their children, and taking care of the weak," Tan Chun added.

Sister Feng laughed. "Tan Chun, are you trying to indulge us? How can trusts be used to take care of the weak?"

"I'm not lying," Tan Chun explained. "If a person has $1 million and his or her wish is to let the poorer child have two-thirds of his assets and the richer child have one-third, that can't be accomplished by a statutory succession where the assets will be equally divided."

She carried on: "However, in the form of a testamentary trust, it would be possible for a trustee to manage and distribute the money according to the grantor's wishes, thus taking care of the weak."

"I heard Pan talking about a real estate trust, too," responded Aunt Xue. "How is that different from what you're talking about?"

Grandmother Jia then commented, chuckling, "It seems that no one is interested in the game today. Everyone is here to take lessons from Tan Chun!"

To learn the difference between the two, you have to read on.

———

HSBC Jintrust investment advisors recommend:

A trust can be used as an instrument of wealth inheritance

Trusts can be broadly classified as self-beneficiary or other-beneficiary. The former refers to a trust for which grantor and beneficiary are the same individual, a trust that benefits the grantor. The latter refers to a trust product for which the grantor and beneficiary are two different individuals. The advantage of the other-beneficiary trust is its capacity to be used as a wealth inheritance vehicle. It is possible for parents to set up a trust that allows their children to receive a fixed amount of money for living expenses every month. Once the inheritance tax is implemented, the affluent families or professionals in the country will be increasingly receptive toward the idea of trusts, and the old saying of "prosperity not surviving past three generations" will be history.

Chapter 26

Comparing Investment Products, Tan Chun Explains Reasons for Poverty

Love for Returns Causes Sister Feng to Forget About Risk

T he last chapter ended with Tan Chun, Grandmother Jia, Sister Feng, and Aunt Xue playing mahjong. Everyone had stopped to listen to Tan Chun talk about the topic of trusts, clearly forgetting their game of mahjong.

On the different trusts, Tan Chun explained, "Presently, capital trusts are the main type of trust product in our country. Trust companies establish trust plans that pool the capital of many individual investors together. The real estate trust that Aunt was talking about belongs to this category."

Grandmother Jia frowned. "How many different types of trusts are there exactly? I'm all confused."

"There is a wide array of diversified trust products; it would be impossible to list them all," Tan Chun giggled. "However, a trust fund is based on using the money pooled from investors to invest; the revenue generated will subsequently be distributed to the investors in proportion to the money invested. Hence, the classification of trust products mainly depends on what the pooled money is invested in. It's called a 'real estate trust' when the funds are invested in real estate; it's called an 'infrastructure trust' when they're invested in the local infrastructure; it's called a 'stock investment trust' when they're invested in securities."

Aunt Xue, teasing Tan Chun, said, "Just look at this mouth of hers; she doesn't stop!"

"Did I say anything wrong?" Tan Chun asked innocently.

"You are always right. But you could have spoken slowly and saved some energy," replied Aunt Xue, laughing.

Sister Feng disagreed. "That's exactly how I like our Tan Chun, unlike those girls who haven't seen the world and speak in weird accents and tones, like mosquitoes humming."

"It would be great if they all settle down to be like you," Grandmother Jia concurred.

Everyone burst into laughter.

Then Sister Feng raised another question: "Since a trust is also a wealth management product, how does it compare to government bonds, funds, and the like?"

"Currently, trust products have an average maturity period of about two years. Compared to other wealth management products, revenue from trust products is higher. For this year, a total of 296 types of trust products were introduced in the country, with an average projected annual yield of 4.6 percent. Although the revenue is lower than for open-ended stock funds, they still fetch higher revenue than bank deposits, government bonds, and currency exchange funds," explained Tan Chun.

Tempted, Sister Feng asked, "How do I buy them?"

Tan Chun chuckled. "When she hears the words 'high return rates,' Sister Feng forgets everything else."

Sister Feng blushed. "True, you're right, Tan Chun. You had better be constantly reminding me because I'm afraid that I won't be able to change this bad habit of mine."

Tan Chun nodded. "Everyone loves high return rates, and the higher the rate, the happier everyone is. It is inevitable. However, do not forget that high return rates and risks are like a pair of twins—they come hand in hand. To enjoy high return rates, you have to bear the high risks."

"So where is the risk in trust products?" asked Sister Feng.

"The risks involved in the operation are fully borne by the investors themselves. The trust companies do not promise intact assets. When a loss is incurred, the company will only hand out compensation when there is a breach of agreement. On another level, although most trust companies are able to fulfill the projected return rates for the trust products, they are, after all, projected rates and not a guaranteed promise."

"In your opinion, how do we avoid risk when deciding on the trust product to invest in?" Sister Feng persisted.

"Firstly, select a reputable trust company. Choose a trustworthy one with strong capital foundations, high reliability, healthy asset conditions, superior staff quality, and good historical performance. Secondly, examine the investment itself—for instance, the industry the investment is based on, the stability and reliability of cash flow of the investment during its operation, and the potential of the trust's market prospects and distribution channels upon initiation. Third is the adequacy of its guarantee measures. Investments that have bank guarantees, bank commitments to repurchase, or provide subsequent loans are usually safer than other trusts."

Grandmother Jia said, "All right, all right, all right, let's talk about something else already. Let's see if the people are all here, and if it's time for us to start the feast." Just as she finished, there was a commotion outside.

To find out what it was about, please continue reading the next chapter.

HSBC Jintrust investment advisors recommend:

Do not consider a projected rate of return to be a promised rate of return

Trusts can also be divided into two classifications: capital trusts and asset trusts. Capital trusts are also known as "cash trusts." The grantor entrusts funds to the trust company. In asset trusts, the grantor entrusts chattel and real estate, including copyrights and other non-currency assets. In China, individual trusts are mainly capital trusts. Trust companies release collective capital trust plans that pool the capital of many individual investors together. The real estate trust that Aunt Xue was talking about belongs to this category.

When purchasing capital trusts, keep in mind that the projected rates of return are still, after all, projections. They are not promises. The trust companies do not promise that your assets will remain intact; the risk of the trust during its operation is wholly borne by the investors.

Chapter 27

Jia Huan is Bitter About a Relatively Small New Year Red Packet

Tan Chun Talks About Blind Comparisons

A s was said, it was Lunar New Year's eve. Tan Chun arrived early and started a game of mahjong with Grandmother Jia, Sister Feng, and Aunt Xue. They were chatting happily when a commotion was heard outside. Listening carefully, Sister Feng deduced that it was Concubine Zhao and little Jia Huan making a din.

Grandmother Jia frowned. "What's with Concubine Zhao this time? Go take a look. Watch that she doesn't teach Jia Huan the wrong things."

Sister Feng hurried out, only to find Jia Huan on the floor wailing and throwing himself about. "With so little red packet money, how can I look good in school?"

Concubine Zhao replied bitterly, "What do you have to complain about? You have only family favoritism to blame!"

Sister Feng hurried to stop her. "It's the New Year! What's happening? Jia Huan is only a child. If he has erred, you should be taking him by the hand and correcting him, not uttering nonsense like that!"

Concubine Zhao did not dare to retort. Sister Feng helped Jia Huan up to his feet and chided him: "You too, boy with such terrible temper! Just how much did your mother give you, that you've to be in such a state?"

"Two hundred dollars," came Jia Huan's hushed reply.

"Even I gave Qiao Jie only $200! What's there to complain about?" Then she turned to get Feng-er. "Fetch my red packet for Jia Huan, and send him to the backyard to play with Lan-er and the rest."

Turning back to Jia Huan, she said sternly to him, "Run along. Don't compare blindly next time!" Jia Huan silently followed Feng-er, received the red packet, and went out to play with Jia Lan and the rest. Concubine Zhao had no choice but to leave, too, murmuring to herself. Sister Feng returned to the room and recounted the incident to Grandmother Jia, Aunt Xue, and Tan Chun.

Grandmother Jia sighed. "This useless troublemaker, being so greedy at this age. What will become of him when he grows up?"

Sister Feng, realizing that the incident involved Tan Chun's mother and younger brother, hurried to defend them. "Seriously, Jia Huan shouldn't be blamed. It's a rat race in school. Having what another person has is a must, and, in fact, it should be better!"

Sister Feng continued: "After school yesterday, Qiao Jie was bugging me to get her a color-screen electronic dictionary, saying that her table partner already has one. I really don't know what to do with her!"

Tan Chun laughed. "There's always a reason for every-thing. Where did Qiao Jie pick up her habit from? Reflect on yourself. Are you also subconsciously comparing Qiao Jie to the other children?"

Sister Feng, after some pondering, answered, "That's true. On occasions when I pick Qiao Jie up from school, if I notice that the other children are more fashionable than she is, I'll take her on a shopping trip immediately. On Qiao Jie's birthday, I let her bring her classmates for a feast. The others have done so, so Qiao Jie also has to do it."

She continued: "I have always been very competitive; I didn't want Qiao Jie to lose to the other children, but have never considered that I might actually be teaching her the wrong values!"

Tan Chun agreed. "You are always comparing, thus subconsciously you actually influenced Qiao Jie, instilling in her the idea that her consumption power is a measure of her ability. Naturally she splurges."

Without waiting for Tan Chun to complete her sentence, Sister Feng agreed. "Exactly! Since, Tan Chun, you were able to explain Qiao Jie's behavior, surely you have a solution?"

Tan Chun replied: "Toward these children who display such lack of judgment when spending, parents should adjust their competitive mentality, and at the same time, cultivate healthy spending habits in their children. Instill the habit of checking out merchandise from different shops. For example, Qiao Jie says, 'The rest of the class have electronic dictionaries that have color displays. I want one too!' At this time, do not agree immediately but instead bring her to the shops to look at the prices of the various brands, the different functions offered by different brands, and the functions that she really needs. Parents can also be the professionals, finding out the varying qualities of the electronic dictionaries of different brands, and then guiding their children along in making the right choice. To encourage healthy spending, parents can implement additional measures, like giving extra money saved to children as pocket money. When the habit of comparing merchandise from various stores is inculcated in the children, they will naturally be more mature and rational when purchasing."

Just as Tan Chun said her piece, the maid came in to announce, "Everyone is here. Do we start the feast?" Upon hearing that, Grandmother Jia ordered that the mahjong set be put away and then asked everyone to take their seats for the feast.

HSBC Jintrust investment advisors recommend:

Correctly influence children's attitudes toward money

Some children spend all their pocket money on food or their favorite toys the moment they lay hands on it. Then, there are some others who will save everything in their piggy banks, not wanting to spend a single cent. Different children's attitudes toward money will, to a certain extent, determine their spending habits in the future. Therefore, it is every parent's responsibility to play a role in guiding their children to have the right mentality toward money.

Chapter 28

Jia Lan Learns Wealth Management Through Fairy Tales

Li Wan Replaces Gift with Savings Account

When everyone was seated, Grandmother Jia started with the introduction: "Since we do not have guests today, please, there's no need to be formal. Do loosen up."

Sister Feng laughed. "The children are waiting for you to give out the red packets. They have been waiting since the beginning of last year. Do you want to send them back with just a meal?"

Grandmother Jia chuckled. "Oh yes, I almost forgot." She turned around to Yuan Yang to get the prepared red packets and handed them out to the children one by one.

Sister Feng joked, "What about us? Well, it seems that no one loves us."

Grandmother Jia replied: "Of course there's a red packet for you." She turned to her maid Yuan Yang and told her, "Come quickly and throw the packet on her." She continued to Sister Feng, "You're certainly not shy. To think Qiao Jie is already entering college soon!" Everyone laughed.

Lady Wang added, "Sister Feng is getting more and more talkative," then gave instructions to the maid to fetch the red packets she had prepared for the children. The red packets were passed around, and the children were delighted.

Grandmother Jia turned around and told Aunt Xue, "When I was their age, my red packet money was only a bit of loose change. Now the money in the red packets is increasing every year."

Aunt Xue agreed. "In the past, the red packets were symbolic of good wishes from elders; now they are valued for practical reasons."

Tan Chun, listening at the side, suggested, "You don't have to give money in red packets. There are other things you could give."

"This is novel. Go on," said Grandmother Jia.

Tan Chun explained: "Red packets could actually help the children to cultivate proper wealth management values. For example, giving wealth management books in the context of fairy tales, though not as direct, is innovative. The children would love it."

Jia Lan nodded as he was filling his plate with the vegetables on the table. "Aunt Tan Chun gave me a book titled *Xiao Gou Qian Qian* only yesterday and I finished reading it all at once. It indeed gave me a clearer knowledge about wealth management."

Sister Feng said, "Is there such a book? Tan Chun should give me one as a gift too; I'll read it with Qiao Jie."

Tan Chun smiled. "This book is considered the world's best wealth management fairy tale, yet it is a suitable read for both adults and children. It is inspiring not only in terms of children's attitudes toward money, but also toward life."

Grandmother Jia asked, "Other than books, what else can we give?"

Tan Chun replied, "Red packets from elders originally symbolized their good wishes for the younger generation. So how about giving an insurance plan, which will be taking actual steps in fulfilling the original intention of giving red packets. By using the red packet money to pay the premium, not only do you help to cultivate the right attitude in the children toward money, but an education endowment could also be established. A sum of educational endowment proportionate to the insured amount can be given at every stage of life."

Sister Feng frowned. "The rate of return for education and endowment insurance is quite low, isn't it?"

"Precisely. Therefore, it cannot be used as the main tool for accumulating educational reserves for your children. What is more important is insuring the risks that the children face at each stage of life. Education and endowment insurance often offers children's medical and accidental mishap insurance at a better price. There are even some forms of insurance that give free 'children's accidental medical insurance' on top of children's education endowment insurance."

Li Wan added: "In my opinion, converting red packets into saving certificates could also be one of the best New Year gifts for the children. A few years ago, I took Lan-er to the bank with the small amount of red packet money he had, and opened an education savings account. The advantage of these savings accounts is, although they work the same way as current savings accounts, they enjoy interest rates of fixed-deposit accounts. In addition, the interest is also tax-exempt. In three years, Lan has saved $20,000 in total; the interest earned is $1,000 more than in a normal current savings account. That is only secondary; the most important gain is having Lan experience the process of saving and understand its benefits even at his young age."

Tan Chun replied with a laugh: "Sister-in-law has always been one step ahead in educating the children about money! This deserves respect."

Just as everyone was enjoying themselves, the maid came in to report, "Granny Liu is here to wish Grand Mistress Jia a happy new year." Grandmother Jia instructed the maid to invite her in immediately.

HSBC Jintrust investment advisors recommend:

Do not use education endowment insurance or educational savings as the only approach to accumulate your children's education endowment

What investment products do we choose when preparing the educational reserves for our children? Do you choose education insurance, educational savings, or open-end funds?

Education endowment and insurance is especially designed by insurance companies to meet the needs of educational fees. The child will receive an amount of educational fees proportionate to the insured value at every stage of life (high school, college, university, starting a business, and so on). The most significant advantage of an education endowment and insurance is that it provides security; the insurance company will cover death, accidents, and health-related risks. However, the return rates are not very high. Currently, children's education insurance has return rates ranging from 1.8 percent to 2.3 percent (not inclusive of any unguaranteed insurance bonus); the liquidity of the funds is low, and the cost to exit after joining is high.

Education savings is one of the many savings categories that enjoy the benefits of two different government incentive policies. Its advantages are that payments are made in the form of installment savings, it enjoys interest rates of fixed deposits, and it is also tax-free. However, the field of investors whose situations are suitable for education savings is narrow. There are also stringent regulations for use of funds. For example, funds in each account must not exceed

$20,000; during the high school, university, and postgraduate years, the investor is able to enjoy tax exemption and interest returns on a maximum of $20,000 in each phase. In other words, an individual will, at most, be able to enjoy this benefit three times. In comparison to the large amount of educational fees, this is only the tip of the iceberg.

Funds, on the other hand, are different. There is a wide spectrum of funds available. There are distinct risks and profit levels for each of them, making it possible to select funds of varying risk, profit, and time span according to the individual household needs and, at the same time, share profits of stock and bond performance in the long run. Moreover, since there is high liquidity, funds can be obtained whenever there is a need.

In general, whether it is savings, insurance, or investment funds, each investment tool has its own unique advantages. Placing all of them in the portfolio especially designed for your child's educational reserve not only reaps revenues, but there is also control over the risks involved without compromising the capacity to accumulate educational fees. However, as a reminder, funds with higher profitability should be used principally; education savings and insurance should play a supporting role. Be careful not to mix up your priorities.

Chapter 29

Granny Liu Brings Laughter Through Pun

Jia Tan Chun Expostulates with the Poor

Granny Liu came into the house leading Ban-er by the hand. She greeted Grandmother Jia and said, "I brought some home-dried beans, tomatoes, and other dried vegetables to show our warm feelings in our meagre way."

Grandmother Jia hurried to assure her: "The people here happen to like dried food. Thank you for taking the time."

Granny Liu laughed. "The ladies must have gotten sick of the delicacies to take a fancy to these. No wonder I've heard that people in the village have started eating fish and meat while the people in the city have gained an appetite for dried vegetables and porridge. I guess we'll never be able to keep pace with the changes anyhow." Everyone laughed in amusement.

While they were talking, the servants set out the cutlery. Granny Liu and Ban-er were invited to join the feast. Upon settling down, Granny Liu noticed that the fully laid out table of dishes was relatively untouched and politely took just a small portion or two from a few dishes. Ban-er, however, at the sight of the food, started to plead with Granny Liu for some meat.

Sister Feng hurried to help Ban-er with the food. "In the blink of an eye, you've grown up! Are you going to high school soon?" asked Sister Feng.

Granny Liu frowned and said, "Don't remind me. This useless monkey wasn't able to get into the best middle schools. His scores were just a few points away. To come up with the school fees, the whole house was thrown into a frenzy. It's also our fault for not planning in advance. This time around we are doing all we can."

Grandmother Jia pointed at Tan Chun and said, "We have a master in wealth management here. Ask her to help you plan!"

Granny Liu waved her hands to decline the offer. "Isn't wealth management a luxury belonging to the affluent? Poor people like us just stick to eating as much rice as we can out of the bowls we own and living our lives honestly. What wealth is there to manage?"

Tan Chun disagreed. "This is where you are wrong. Wealth management is really the way you earn, save, and spend money. The importance of wealth management has nothing to do with your financial ability, but is an objective of family life. Don't you wish to let Ban-er go to a better high school? It is even more vital to manage your money well when there isn't much. In this way, the limited resources can be put to maximum use."

Granny Liu nodded. "I see. Learning the techniques of wealth management is like understanding how to cook a pot of tasty porridge even with only a little rice. It's just that families like ours have so little. How do we manage our wealth?"

Tan Chun laughed. "Wealth management doesn't necessarily require large investments. There are many methods for managing your wealth according to your financial ability. With just a little money, you can invest in products that have small requirements and are easy to cash out. For instance, funds are available from $1,000 onward. If it's a regular fixed-amount fund, a starting investment can be as low as $200. In short, choose an investment method that is suitable for yourself, allow excess money to start moving, and in a while, it will start accumulating."

For a moment, Granny Liu hadn't come around to understand what Tan Chun was saying and mistook the "funds" mentioned as "chicken essence" because the two Chinese terms sound similar. She stuck out her tongue in bemusement. "Wow, just what sort of chicken essence is it that's so expensive and warrants $1,000 to buy?" Upon hearing this, everyone roared with laughter.

Tan Chun contained her laughter, saying, "It's not chicken essence. It may sound the same, but the two Chinese characters are not the same."

Grandmother Jia asked: "I've heard you speak so much about funds, but what exactly are the benefits?"

Tan Chun explained: "A fund is like a huge pouch with many people putting their money in it. The money in this pouch is placed in the hands of professionals in fund management companies to invest in stocks or bonds."

"I can buy the stocks on my own, so is there a need to go through these companies?" asked Grandmother Jia.

Tan Chun replied: "The most significant difference between buying stocks directly and buying through a fund is the ability to achieve great results with little money. For example, you can only buy, at most, one or two types of shares if you decide to use $1,000 to buy stocks on your own. On the other hand, buying a fund with $1,000 in reality means buying over 10 different types of shares. In this way, you enjoy the benefits of dispersing your investments and lowering the overall risk."

Grandmother Jia nodded. "What you said is true. But how do I know if the fund management company can be trusted?"

HSBC Jintrust investment advisors recommend:

Wealth management is not a game just for the rich

Wealth management requires intelligence and is not a game for just the rich. People of middle to low income have little starting capital, lower risk tolerance, and generally lack real experience. In spite of these issues, by paying special attention to the following points, the goal of successfully managing wealth can still be reached.

Firstly, cultivate a healthy perspective on wealth management investments. Wealth management is all about managing personal and family finances in order to reach a higher objective in life. Therefore, do not be too concerned with the input–output ratio; as long as the goal is met through wealth management, it is considered a success.

Secondly, correct your understanding of risks. People of middle to low income have lower risk tolerance. However, do be conscious that risks and profits are directly proportional. Blindly avoiding risks and shying away the moment risks are slightly higher will only bring you returns of fixed deposit rates without any wealth management to speak of.

Thirdly, seek the advice of professionals. Investment advisors, with rich experience and adequate information, are trustworthy. Employing the service of a professional to assist in wealth management through investing in funds, especially for small investors, can double the results. Never invest blindly.

Chapter 30

Brave Bao Yu is a Risk Taker

Cautious Granny Liu is Risk Averse

In the last chapter, Grandmother Jia enquired about what makes a fund management company trustworthy.

Tan Chun answered: "You become a fund holder when you purchase a fund. Your money will be converted to a certain number of fund units, and they, together with the other fund holders' units, make up the assets of the fund. A professional team from the fund management company will make use of these assets to finance the purchase of stocks and bonds, forming the fund's investment portfolio. The shares that you hold are a miniature copy of this investment portfolio. Since the fund's assets are independently entrusted to the bank, that bank will oversee the investments made by the company. Moreover, the China Securities Regulatory Commission's regulation of trust funds has become extremely strict; operation of fund companies can be said to be completely transparent. With the frequent updates that the fund provides, you will be very clear about the operating conditions of the fund." Grandmother Jia nodded in silence as she listened.

Bao Yu asked, "What makes you think the fund managers would be better than we are? I beg to differ; I feel that it would be better to speculate on our own, to watch the stocks rise. How thrilling!"

Dai Yu smiled and, poking fun at Bao Yu, said, "You don't say! The stock index has been rising for some time, but the stocks you bought were motionless. Thrilling? I would say, chilling!"

Bao Yu chuckled. "What did I do? Why are you ridiculing me?" He continued: "You don't understand. I bought small cap technology stocks, but recently, it has been the large cap blue chips that have been skyrocketing. Who would have expected that even elephants could dance?"

"Exactly. On your own, you can only invest in five or six different equities. There is no way of spreading out the risk. In a fund portfolio, where many more different equities are invested in, there will surely be a few profitable shares. Moreover, it has become increasingly tricky for individual speculators, since there are growing numbers of equities and factors that influence market performance. For example, the rise and fall of the price of oil, the central banks changing interest rates, the fluctuation of exchange rates, and so on will all affect the local stock market. How can the average retail investor manage to keep track of all these?" Tan Chun asked.

Bao Yu nodded. "That's true. I'm unarmed. How do I triumph over those organizational investors who spend day and night researching? We should just let funds buy equities for us!"

Granny Liu, who was listening in awe, suddenly understood. "So this fund helps us to invest in equities? Doesn't this mean that there will be risks? How can poor people like us bear the risk?"

Tan Chun said reassuringly, "Granny, you're perfectly right. People with lower income have lower tolerance for risk, but don't forget that risks and profits are inseparable. Steering completely clear of risk would mean avoiding chances of high profits, too. If you only guard your bank savings, you will face another kind of risk—the devaluation of your money due to inflation, and this is actually the most terrifying kind of risk."

Granny Liu nodded in approval.

Tan Chun continued: "Another thing. A slight difference in the rate of return, which may not seem much to you now, will in fact make a huge difference in the long run. Take, for instance, two available investment plans; the first one has an annual profit of 10 percent and the second has an annual profit of 7 percent. Both require a commitment of $1,000 monthly for 30 years. Although it is only a difference of 3 percent, in 30 years, the former plan will reap an investment profit of $2,260,000 and the latter a profit of $1,220,000—a difference of a million dollars!"

Granny Liu shook her head in disbelief. "Good gracious! Today's 3 percent difference translates into a difference of a million in 30 years! I had better take some risk now even if the rate of return is only a few percentage points higher."

Sister Feng laughed. "Tan Chun must be muddle-headed! Just the other day, you were advising me against pursuing higher profit rates and forgetting about risks, and now you're telling Granny Liu to bear more risks. Aren't you contradicting yourself now?"

HSBC Jintrust investment advisors recommend:

Bearing a moderate amount of risk will bring higher rates of return

Risks and returns are inseparable. Avoiding risks completely would mean avoiding chances of higher return rates. Moreover, even a slight disparity in rates of return will snowball into a huge difference in accumulated wealth before you realize it.

Consider two available investment plans; both require a commitment of $1,000 monthly for 30 years, the first one has an annual

profit of 10 percent and the second has an annual profit of 7 percent.
You may not be concerned about a 3 percent difference. However,
a difference of 3 percent in 30 years translates into the former plan
reaping an investment profit of $2,260,000 and the latter a profit of
$1,220,000. You will be shortchanging yourself over $1,000,000!
So if there were a chance of earning 10 percent, why would you
want to stop at 7 percent?

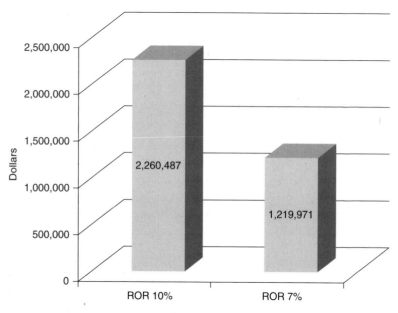

Figure 30.1 Return comparison

Of course, we must first determine if the risk of an investment
is moderate. Moderate risk-taking means that even if the investment fails, it will not threaten the more important personal or
family goals, such as livelihood, the education of the children, and
retirement. If you're still young and healthy, and already starting
to accumulate a retirement fund, invest in stocks and be bold in
bearing a little more risk in order to get higher return rates.

Chapter 31

Sensible Village Woman Considers Investment

Worried About Retirement, Jia Zheng Buys Antiques

In the previous chapter, Tan Chun advised Granny Liu to bear a little more risk in order to receive higher returns. Sister Feng interrupted: "Tan Chun must be muddle-headed! A little while ago, you were advising me against pursuing higher rates of profit and forgetting about risks, and now you're telling Granny Liu to bear more risks. Aren't you contradicting yourself now?"

Tan Chun explained, laughing: "Sister Feng, you're testing me again. You only know the first part of the story. It is never good to have too much of anything. It's true that we should not overlook possible risks in our investments, but it is also important that we are not overly conservative. The key is the investment period and your tolerance for risk."

"That differs in each individual, right?" said Sister Feng.

Tan Chun nodded. "Yes. If you're saving up Qiao Jie's university fees for next year, you naturally cannot take too much risk. On the other hand, if Granny Liu is saving Ban-er's university fees that are due in six or seven years, why not take a little higher risk?"

Granny Liu sighed. "It's no wonder we weren't able to make it rich. It's because we do not know these essential truths. We wasted all those years! When I return home, I must urge my sons and daughters-in-law to make some investments. Then there will not be a need to worry about Ban-er's future educational needs."

Ban-er was happily and busily eating away, but upon hearing his name, with his mouth still full of food, he said loudly, "The food today is especially tasty!"

Granny Liu, disappointed and annoyed, slapped Ban-er in the face and chided, "You useless thing, instead of learning the right things, all you know is how to eat!"

Ban-er was about to burst into tears when everyone played mediator to calm Granny Liu down.

"Since we have just eaten, let's go out for a stroll and come back later," Grandmother Jia suggested when the food was finished.

Thereupon, everyone stood up from their seats and followed Grandmother Jia into the yard to enjoy the fireworks display. Tan Chun, suddenly remembering that she had yet to pay New Year respects to her father, Jia Zheng, decided to leave the crowd for the study, where she thought Jia Zheng must be.

As she made a turn on the path, a man in high spirits almost ran right into her. The man came to a stop. "Happy New Year, Miss Tan Chun!"

On closer inspection, Tan Chun realized that it was the general manager of Jin Ling Antique Company, Leng Zi Xing. She asked, "What brings the ever-busy Mr. Leng here?"

Leng Zi Xing laughed. "Today, the Master has especially called for me. I wouldn't dare not come."

Tan Chun mused, "What has my father called on you for?"

"The Master is quite a generous spender. He has placed orders for quite a few of the antique calligraphy and paintings I brought with me!"

This news troubled Tan Chun and she hurried to end the conversation to look for her father. "I'll talk to you another day. Is it all right if I don't see you off?" Leng Zi Xing made his way out without another word.

When Tan Chun arrived at the study, she saw Jia Zheng pacing up and down the room. After paying her respects, she asked, "What has happened to put you in such a good mood as to buy artwork?"

Jia Zheng sighed. "It's just that I'm nearing retirement age and getting quite sick of the politics at work, so I'm planning for the future."

"Art is a rarely used investment method that requires expertise and skill. If you lack the appreciation skills and end up buying fakes, that would result in complete losses!" Tan Chun said worriedly. "Have you been studying how to become an art connoisseur?"

Jia Zheng shook his head. "I merely do it as a hobby. I do know a little."

"If that's the case," Tan Chun mused aloud, "buying a few paintings because you appreciate them is enough. You will have to be extremely careful of the risks involved if you're thinking of using this as an investment tool for value preservation and growth."

Puzzled, Jia Zheng asked, "As long as it's the real deal, it will naturally increase in value. What's the risk?"

Disagreeing, Tan Chun said, "Even if it's a masterpiece, over-speculation could lead to far-fetched prices. I'm afraid that it's not always profitable." Continuing, she said, "It is not unprecedented, and there have been examples in other countries. For instance, Girl Before a Mirror by Picasso fetched a price of $24 million at a New York auction house in 1989. In the mid-1990s, the selling price dropped to $18.2 million. The investor lost almost $6 million."

Jia Zheng, after listening to Tan Chun's advice, hesitated before asking, "Well, in your opinion, how should I be investing?"

HSBC Jintrust investment advisors recommend:

Only invest in fields you are familiar with

Every successful person has a specific field of expertise. Take, for instance, Tiger Woods; you can be apathetic towards sports in general, but you will definitely be able to name his field of expertise. Do you believe Tiger Woods could be as aggressive as a tiger on the basketball court? Unlikely.

Success cannot be divorced from specialization and it is the same in the investment sector. Successful investors place all their attention on a small group of investment targets and are clear about what they know and what they do not. As a reminder, "knowledge" and "understanding" are different matters; "knowledge" usually refers to the aggregation of facts—"the total of information that is already known to a person"—but "understanding" is the union of knowledge and experience, the ability to employ information to meet a desired result. Art is a very unconventional investment, also known as an alternative investment. It requires a high level of expertise and skill. Lacking the professional skills for appreciation can result in costly consequences. There is no harm if you're buying a few pieces of art because you like them, but if you are using this investment to achieve value preservation and growth, as an amateur, you will have to be very careful of the risks involved. Suitably lower the proportion of your artwork investment. It would be best to limit it to 10 percent.

Chapter 32

Muddle-Headed Man Naively Purchases Gold

Intelligent Daughter Categorizes Assets

I n the prior chapter, when Tan Chun heard that Jia Zheng had ordered many pieces of antique calligraphy and paintings from Leng Zi Xing, she hurried to the study to advise Jia Zheng against it. "If you are serious about artwork investment, you'll have to look at it in the long run. Artwork is not suitable for short-term investment; it requires patience for the price to appreciate."

Jia Zheng asked, "So how long do you think the investment term should be?"

"Generally speaking, about 10 years would be a reasonable investment term," Tan Chun replied.

Disappointed, Jia Zheng said, "Forget it, then. I was originally thinking of garnering some retirement funds through this investment."

"Also," continued Tan Chun, "Father, you're, after all, not well-versed in this area, so you should try to keep the investment in artwork to at most 10 percent of your total investments."

"The amount of assets I have invested in artwork is very little; I invested slightly more in gold, and these two investments together make up one-third of my total investments. Another third is invested in US dollars. The remaining third is in bank deposits."

Tan Chun, unsettled by what her father had said, exclaimed, "This is not good! Although gold is great as a way to store wealth, the growing trend of investing in gold for speculation has been causing fluctuations that are greater than in previous years, thus increasing the risk of investing in gold."

She continued: "Then again, of the available gold investments, paper gold or gold bars are still most practical. You initially invested in gold to fight rising inflation. Using 10 percent of your assets to purchase gold bars would be enough. Now one-third of your assets are in works of art and gold, which are investments with high risk and low liquidity."

"Another one-third—your investment in US dollars—is exposed to the risk of fluctuating exchange rates. In the case of major fluctuations in prices of artworks or the sudden appreciation of the currency, a large part of your assets will face the risk of shrinking. For your age, this is a bit too risky," Tan Chun concluded.

Jia Zheng stroked his moustache in deep thought for a moment, and asked, "Then how do you think I should invest to ensure that I can put my mind at ease during my retirement?"

"Why don't you borrow the concept of core and satellite assets? In addition to giving you better control of risks, it can also help you to achieve higher profit margins. Core assets making up 70 percent to 80 percent of your total investments could be used to achieve mid- to long-term financial goals—for example, retirement, or educational fees for the children. When investing in core assets, you should be concerned about stability and consider the returns in the mid to long run," Tan Chun suggested.

"On the other hand, your satellite assets, which make up 20 percent to 30 percent of your investments, can be used to fulfill luxurious wants like a vacation overseas. The investment proportion of satellite assets is small so it wouldn't cause much harm in case of a loss. Therefore, investments made with satellite assets can be of higher risk; you can even buy high and sell low with them," she said.

Jia Zheng agreed. "Makes sense. It looks like I'll have to lower the proportion of investment in artwork and US dollars to within 20 percent. At the same time, the investments for my retirement fund should be drawn from the core assets. I will have to look out for an investment category that is able to fend off inflation, yet at the same time maintains my principal. It's not so easy."

Tan Chun laughed. "This is nothing difficult. I just recommended funds to Granny Liu. They are very suitable for core asset investments. You can build a fund portfolio with fixed-period and fixed-amount investments, and it is not only possible to stave off inflation in the mid to long run but the risk taken is also within a reasonable range."

"I also heard that there are many types of funds with unique individual characteristics. It is best to invest in a portfolio of funds," Jia Zheng added.

Tan Chun then proposed, "You may choose to invest in equity funds, and at the same time, buy some bond funds and currency funds. In most cases, when the stock market is doing badly, bond funds perform well. They serve as a cushion. In a bull market, the equity funds can also contribute. For daily reserves at home, we can replace them with currency funds.

HSBC Jintrust investment advisors recommend:

Distinguish between core and satellite assets

Introducing the concept of core and satellite assets can help you control your investment risks and produce higher profits. What are core assets? They are what you use to achieve important mid- to long-term financial goals, such as children's education fees, retirement income, or a first home. Core assets normally make up 70 percent to 80 percent of assets. Investments made with core assets should be mid to long term, very systematic, and stable. More attention should be paid to strong, stable rewards in the mid to long term.

For luxuries like vacations, you may use 20 percent to 30 percent of your assets as satellite assets. The main purpose of the satellite assets is to earn more investment returns by bearing higher investment risks. This will not affect some established financial needs, like retirement income and educational fees, in case of investment loss. To put it simply, investing satellite assets is relatively flexible; you may choose investment products of higher risk or even try to capture the market's opportunistic timings and hot spots.

Chapter 33

Aunt Xue Wants to Buy Treasury Bonds

Tan Chun Visits and Solves an Enigma

In the last chapter, Tan Chun suggested that Jia Zheng divide his assets into core and satellite assets. Core assets could be used to invest in a portfolio designed to meet retirement needs. Jia Zheng thought about Tan Chun's suggestion and agreed: "All right, we'll do it your way then. You have gained much from your trip to America. Do visit your Brother Bao Yu when you're free and add to his knowledge." Tan Chun quickly bowed to agree, and carried on chatting with her father about daily family affairs before finally taking her leave.

We'll fast forward to after the Lantern Festival. Tan Chun had heard from Lady Wang that Aunt Xue had fallen ill, and she intended to visit her. She just reached the Xues' front gate as Bao Chai was personally seeing a physician out.

183

When she saw Tan Chun, Bao Chai smiled. "I haven't seen you for a long time! How have you been?"

Tan Chun, returning the friendly gesture, replied, "Fine. How about you?"

After Bao Chai had sent the physician off, the two girls stood in the yard for a talk.

"On the last day before the New Year, Aunt Xue was looking good. Why has she suddenly become ill?"

Bao Chai sighed and said, "It's all the treasury bonds' fault." She explained: "Since her retirement, my mum has become a hard-core fan of treasury bonds. Whenever they are issued, she will get my brother to help her buy some. But just a few days ago, brother went to buy some goods at Yi Wu and took Xiang Ling with him. I was also away on a business trip. My mum had no choice but to make a trip down herself, bringing the maid along."

She continued: "Little did anyone expect that they were so popular this time round that she didn't manage to buy any, even though she was there early. Having stood out in the open for nothing the whole morning, she felt all giddy when she returned home. She seemed all right at first, but for the past few days, it hasn't been good. So I sent for the physician."

Tan Chun was about to say something when Aunt Xue's voice could be heard from inside the house, "Who's here?"

Tan Chun lifted the curtains to enter the room and paid her respects. Aunt Xue, who was lying in bed, sat up and asked Bao Chai to get a pillow to prop her up. Gratified, Aunt Xue said, "I never imagined you would come on such a freezing day. I was just thinking of asking Bao Chai to invite you over; it's such a coincidence that you came."

Tan Chun sat down on the edge of the bed. "What's the matter? What are you worrying about, even though you're sick?"

Chuckling, Aunt Xue said, "Well, it's nothing. I am just upset over not being able to buy any treasury bonds this time round. So I am thinking of letting you, the wealth management expert, give me ideas on what other investment methods may be suitable for me."

She elaborated: "I do not ask for a high rate of return; it's good enough as long as it's better than the average bank deposits."

Tan Chun replied, "The risk of investing in treasury bonds is low, they have stable profits, and the interest is tax-exempt. It is indeed a very suitable option for conservative investors like you. However, that doesn't mean that there is no risk in invest-ing in treasury bonds. For example, if the central bank decides to increase the interest, the returns you get from the treasury bonds might even be lower than the interest earned from bank deposits of the same duration. Also, the treasury bonds that you buy over the bank counters are non-transferable. There are also handling charges for premature withdrawal of investments. Should you be in sudden need of money, you would have to suffer in silence."

Aunt Xue replied, "Yes, but I've also heard from people that there's a type of treasury bond that is tradable. Is it true?"

"That's different from the treasury bonds that you bought. This type of bond does not have a bond certificate, but instead records the data in the bank account using a computer system. You will be able to hold these treasury bonds till they are due, or you can take advantage of the changes and projections of interest rates to buy or sell them. For example, if the interest rates are projected to rise, you may sell your bonds, or if they are falling, you can purchase more," explained Tan Chun.

Aunt Xue creased her forehead. "Does this other type of trea-sury bond have higher risk?"

Tan Chun nodded. "Exactly. Since you do not like risks, this product might not be suitable."

"Why not invest in a principal-guaranteed fund to replace your investment in treasury bonds?" Tan Chun suggested, and continued, "This type of fund has a breakeven period, which is normally three years. After the breakeven period, not only does it guarantee that your original investment is safe, but it also gives you a chance to enjoy returns that are higher than bank deposits and treasury bonds."

Aunt Xue asked doubtfully, "Are you sure there's such a fund? You're not just trying to humor me, right?"

"This is for real," defended Tan Chun, "but if it is redeemed before the breakeven period, not only is it not guaranteed that you will keep your principal investment, but you will also have to pay a higher redemption fee."

Aunt Xue replied, "That's okay. I'd have to hold the national debts for just as long."

HSBC Jintrust investment advisors recommend:

Refrain from investing in products of similar risk/return characteristics

When selecting wealth management products, do not look at them solely from the perspective of product variety. Instead, consider your asset portfolio and allocation to choose products of varying risk/return characteristics. By going for only products of similar risk/return characteristics, you will not be able to effectively diversify investment product types, and consequently spread the risk involved. Take, for example, fixed deposits and bonds. Both of these investments have a certain level of risk tied to interest rates. When the interest rates increase, the returns of both of these two investments will suffer hidden losses. However, if the portfolio includes a currency fund, or a hybrid fund that includes other investment types to spread out the risk, the effect the interest rates have on the assets will be reduced.

Chapter 34

Bao Chai Does Her Best to Manage the Fund

Tan Chun Suggests Personalization

In the preceding chapter, when Tan Chun came to visit Aunt Xue, she mentioned that a principal-guaranteed fund could replace Aunt Xue's investment in the treasury bonds. Tan Chun said, "This fund heavily invests its assets in bonds, so guarantees the security of the principal investment within the breakeven period." Tan Chun further elaborated: "The remainder is sparingly invested in equities, financial derivative products, and other high-profit financial investments to boost the potential of returns, allowing investors to enjoy profits from the stock market on the basis of having secured principal investments. However, the disadvantage of this is that in situations like a bull market, there will be an opportunity cost of being unable to profit more due to the small investment in equities."

Aunt Xue replied, "It's okay. Age is catching up with me. I won't be able to deal with the ups and downs of the stock market."

After some casual talk, Tan Chun, noticing that Aunt Xue was getting tired, said, "Aunt, you must be exhausted, do rest well, I'll go outside to see what Bao Chai is doing."

"Yes, yes. You two haven't seen each other for some time. She must be in the room outside. Run along," said Aunt Xue.

Tan Chun got off the bed. The moment she lifted the curtains of the door between the two rooms, she saw Bao Chai leaning against the table and reading away in the next room. Chuckling, Tan Chun teased, "It's the weekend, yet Sister Bao Chai is so hardworking." She took a step forward to take a closer look. "What book are you reading?"

"Oh, I randomly picked this up from the bookshelf," Bao Chai said, laughing. "It's something about private fund investment."

"You're not in charge of finance in the company. Why are you reading this?" asked Tan Chun curiously.

Bao Chai heaved a sigh, then said, "Have you forgotten that year when your house was divvying up the assets, Old Lady Jia instructed that every household has to contribute a portion of money every year to set up a risk fund? I was put in charge of it."

She continued: "In recent years, this money has snowballed and I hadn't dared to do any high-risk investment, but only buy treasury bonds. My mother learned about the treasury bonds from me."

"Good job!" applauded Tan Chun. "Sister Bao Chai has become a private fund manager!"

"I'm only following instructions. Can't you see that I'm distressed? Instead of helping me, you're teasing me! See that I don't pinch your cheek!" Bao Chai pressed Tan Chun on the bed and was about pinch her when Tan Chun pleaded through laughter, "Good sister! Please spare me! I won't do it again!"

"All right, I'll let you off, but on the condition that you contribute a suggestion. I'm not an expert in investments; I won't be able to meet Old Lady Jia's expectation of 'profiting with never a loss' no matter how much I worry. If there is any mistake, I'll lose all the benefits I have."

Tan Chun sat up, tidied her hair, and said, "Precisely. I suggest that you'd better let the external professional investment institutions manage the money."

"I wish I could. However, the investment products in the market now are all principally public offerings, gathering many investors' money to make a standardized investment. It will not be possible to meet our personalized needs for this risk fund," said Bao Chai, "I'm not able to put my mind at ease with this private fund."

"That's true," Tan Chun replied, then paused for a long while before getting a new idea. "Why not this," she said excitedly, "Hand it over to the fund management company to have a specialized wealth management account, and you might as well job hop over to become a specialized account fund manager!"

"I just spared you a moment ago and you're at it again!" Bao Chai gritted her teeth and got ready to pinch Tan Chun.

Tan Chun made her escape and said, "Okay, let's get serious. Personalized wealth management is actually a package of investment advisory services. All of the investors have their own independent accounts, and the investment plans are all tailored to meet the specific needs of each investor to reach different investment aims."

"Doesn't sound like a bad idea," said Bao Chai, "but this fund of ours might not be able to meet the lowest criteria for having personalized wealth management."

Tan Chun replied, "Not necessarily. I heard that the China Securities Regulatory Commission is discussing specific matters concerning the fund management companies; the minimum requirement of a single transaction is estimated to be around the level of tens of millions. Moreover, the lower limit of foreign personalized wealth management is getting progressively lower, so who knows if we won't fulfill the criteria?"

Bao Chai nodded and said, "All right, enough of this. Since there's no one else here today, I have something else to ask you and you have to answer truthfully."

Puzzled, Tan Chun asked, "What do you want to ask?"

You have to read on to know what happened next.

HSBC Jintrust investment advisors recommend:

The elderly should lower their expectations when managing their wealth

In the course of wealth management, the silver generation often complain that although savings deposits and buying treasury bonds (T-bills) are the preferred methods of wealth management, the savings returns are still relatively low and even more dismal after taxation. Moreover, the maturity periods for T-bills are longer than suitable for investors of the silver generation.

These traditional wealth management methods are increasingly unable to meet their needs. The elderly are now more prone to choosing investment methods that have high profit returns, which are fast rewarding, and at the same time, do not require too much capital or effort. These, however, in reality, are often unattainable.

In actual fact, the elderly person's main objective in wealth management should not be high returns, but instead, they should humble their expectations to beating the annual rate of inflation, which means not letting their assets shrink by too much. That will be completing the first step to success. Of course, it is also vital to actively learn and grasp the latest wealth management dynamics. For example, though there is not much difference in the security of currency funds and bank deposits, returns from currency funds are higher, and the encashment is also more flexible, making it a good replacement for fixed deposits; principal-guaranteed funds allow investors to enjoy profits from stocks on the basis of a secure principal fund, and they are thus also a good to treasury bonds.

Inability and unwillingness of the elderly to renew perspective and accept new things will most probably cause them to miss out on these investment varieties.

Chapter 35

Tan Chun Talks About Her Concerns

Grandmother Jia Holds Another Contest

In the previous chapter, Tan Chun and Bao Chai were talking in the house when Bao Chai suddenly asked, "I have something to ask you. Are you hiding anything from me and the other girls? Just speak the truth."

Tan Chun replied, "What could I be hiding? I haven't been out all this time."

"Stop pretending already. Ying-er heard from Cui Mo that though you haven't been going out, you've been receiving many letters. Also international calls every two or three days, and each call has been never-ending."

Blushing, Tan Chun said, "Well, what else do you want me to say if you already know about it?"

Bao Chai probed further. "Where exactly is your 'foreign friend' from?" She continued: "I remember one year when your brother Bao Yu celebrated his birthday, we went to the temple to ask for a divination lot together for fun. You got one with the message 'the person who receives this lot will marry a rich husband.' Has it come true?"

Looking around to make sure there was no one around, Tan Chun lowered her voice. "I shall only tell you," she said, whispering. "He was my classmate at Harvard. I didn't know his family background then, only that we mutually liked each other. Upon my return, I received a letter from him saying that he is actually the prince of Denmark. Now this makes me hesitate; which of those royal grandchildren are not fickle?"

"It doesn't matter! You should know each other's temperament after spending so much time together at Harvard. What is there to worry about?"

Tan Chun nodded. "Well, that's true, he is very sincere; he has already told his parents about us, and when they come over to the capital for a state visit, they will be coming to our house to ask for my hand in marriage."

Bao Chai laughed. "He must be destined to be your rich husband! But Old Lady Jia might be alarmed because she didn't expect Westerners as in-laws!"

Before they could finish their talk, the maid said from outside the room, "Old Lady Jia has invited both you ladies over. She said that it was urgent."

Bao Chai nudged Tan Chun. "Hurry over to meet your future in-laws!"

Observing that Tan Chun wasn't moving, she said, "Are you feeling shy again? Should you be required to do state visits like Princess Diana, are you going to use shyness as an excuse not to go?" Saying that, she shoved Tan Chun out and into Grandmother Jia's room.

Sister Feng, Bao Yu, Dai Yu, Ying Chun, Xi Chun, Xiang Yun, and the others were there, too. The two of them, after paying respects to Grandmother Jia, went on to greet the girls. Tan Chun glanced at the heap of Western goods piled up in the corner of the room and knew in her heart that the people of Denmark had come and left. However, Tan Chun, unable to detect Grandmother Jia's mood through her facial expressions, felt very uneasy.

Grandmother Jia said, "I did some math. It has been about a year since Tan Chun returned. I hear that she hasn't been wasting any time at all. She has been busy playing the role of financial advisor for all of you in the house."

She continued: "Now I want all of you to tell me what you have learned. The best answers will, like the last time, receive a reward from me."

Bao Chai replied, "May I request that the reward this time not to be tuition fees for Harvard in the US? I was thinking more of a trip to Europe."

"Old Lady Jia is asking a serious question. Don't digress!" said Tan Chun.

"Let me go first," said Sister Feng, "Although I was in charge of managing the house, I knew nothing about wealth management, causing the household to almost disintegrate. I am still very sorry about that incident. All thanks to Tan Chun, after hearing her opinions, I now understand that in wealth management, planning is of the greatest importance. First, calculate one's financial situation and find out how much can be used in investments. What is your asset liability and what can you use when you need money? Knowing yourself, what is your level of interest in taking risk—are you conservative, aggressive, or stable? Who are the family members, and what are the future expenditures of the children, such as education endowments and daily expenses? What do you expect of the living standards and conditions during your twilight years? Clarify these questions before considering investment methods to meet your objectives. Because there is information all over the place, with no overall planning, you will be sure to commit the mistake I made."

To learn more, read on.

HSBC Jintrust investment advisors recommend:

There must be planning before an investment

Inventory your financial properties. Do you find that your investment decisions were too diversified? On hearing about X stocks, do you hurry to purchase them? When Uncle comes with "insider information" that a dreadful policy will be unveiled the next day, do you hurry to sell the stocks? In the end, you realize that you're all confused. Neither depending on yourself nor listening to others has made your final investment results satisfactory; perhaps you should just leave it in the hands of luck? Of course not!

It is vital to have an overall plan of asset allocation, and not have your investments scattered all over the place. However, as a normal investor trying to come up with a comprehensive investment plan, there might be some areas that you will be unable to take care of. In such situations, you should seek advice from experts.

Chapter 36

Tan Chun Marries Abroad

Dai Yu Ends the Story with a New Poem

I n the preceding chapter, Grandmother Jia called to assemble everybody and instructed each person to share their year's experience regarding wealth management. The person with the best answer would get a prize.

Sister Feng had given a long speech about the importance of planning in wealth management. Grandmother Jia smiled and asked, "Another question. I heard that you opened a structured deposit account for making periodic payment investments for Qiao Jie. How are the returns?"

Sister Feng laughed. "A periodic payment plan is a long-term investment. Though it takes little effort and time, a few years will be required to see the results of accumulation. It has only been about a year. I'm not counting my returns yet."

"Old Lady Jia was merely testing you," Bao Chai interrupted. "In the beginning, the only thing on your mind was returns, but now your willingness to be a long-term investor shows that you've finally understood."

Sister Feng laughed. "If I still didn't show any improvement, I would be the most backward person in the Grand Garden. I wouldn't think of living here anymore." Everyone laughed.

Li Wan was next to speak. "In my opinion, the most important thing in wealth management is to make sure that there is proper asset allocation. Allocate different proportions of your assets to different investment categories based on your age and risk-tolerance level."

Grandmother Jia commented, "That is another deep opinion, but it's easier said than done, right?"

Li Wan giggled. "Precisely. That was why I felt that investment and wealth management should be left to the professionals. For instance, in raising the fees for Lan's education abroad, I bought a life-cycle fund and allowed the fund manager to adjust the asset allocation. All I have to do is make sure that Lan studies hard."

Grandmother Jia cautioned, "Hasn't Lan just gotten some Math Olympiad award? He's still young. Don't stress him too much." Li Wan nodded in agreement.

Xi Chun said, "Sister Tan Chun has taught us a lot. There's one particular lesson that I find very true: to profit from investments, it is necessary to start early. I have started investing, so that in the future I may retire early to travel around the world."

Bao Chai laughed. "Wouldn't your fans be terribly depressed if you stopped drawing?"

Xi Chun, amused, said, "How can my fan base be compared to Sister Dai Yu's? Her new poetry anthology has received very good reviews from critics." Dai Yu smiled at Xi Chun's comment without responding.

Dejected, Bao Yu sighed, "All of you are faring so well now. I'm the only one who hasn't benefitted. I once heeded Tan Chun's advice to build an investment portfolio, but forgot all about it when I was helping Dai Yu with her poetry anthology. When I remembered and checked on it yesterday, I was surprised that one of the shares has even been delisted."

Tan Chun replied, "I've said that there must be regular assessment in investments. But you only have Dai Yu's matters on your mind. Everything else is of no importance to you." Bao Yu smiled playfully.

Everyone else said something about his or her learnings. Grandmother Jia raised her voice, "Let me do the judging. In general, all of you have made improvements since the beginning, with only Bao Yu slightly off the mark. Since you've all done well, I'll invite all of you on a trip to Denmark for a vacation."

Everyone was shocked. Sister Feng asked excitedly, "Why are you spending so much? Have you won the lottery?"

Grandmother laughed. "All right, I shall speak the truth. This is all due to Tan Chun." She proceeded to tell the story of Denmark's prince asking for Tan Chun's hand in marriage, and added, "Our Western in-laws have invited us to Tan Chun's wedding, and all of you will have a chance to share the limelight."

The girls congratulated Tan Chun. Tan Chun, with her face flushed, bowed her head and played with her belt in an attempt to hide her embarrassment.

Xiang Yun, nudging Bao Yu, teased, "You were the last today, so you won't be able to come along."

Bao Yu got panicky and pleaded with Grandmother Jia. Grandmother chuckled. "You can go, but you'll be punished by carrying the bags when your sisters are shopping." Everyone laughed and concurred that it wasn't a bad idea. Bao Yu's happiness was written all over his face.

Grandmother Jia said, "On this trip, Tan Chun, you mustn't forget about gaining experience in investment overseas. In the future, continue to teach your family here."

Tan Chun replied, "Naturally I will." She continued, "Actually, I have written down everyone's experience in investment as stories in a book. This will be different from the articles of the professionals. It will give readers a fresh perspective and understanding of the theories of investment." Saying that, she took out a book and handed it to Grandmother Jia.

Everyone flipped through it and was full of praise. Dai Yu said, "Tan Chun's book talks about the Red Chamber with a brand new story. Why not name it *Wealth Management of the Red Chamber*? I'll compose a poem to end the story." She followed with:

> *Revel in the new Red Chamber*
> *Let the tales of investment intrigue*
> *And all financial puzzles be solved*
> *Now financial freedom is a dream no more!*

HSBC Jintrust investment advisors recommend:

There must be regular assessment of your investment portfolio

Investment is only a beginning. However, many investors fail to remember this; after selecting a certain investment distribution or building an investment portfolio, they lose the alertness and sharpness they had in the beginning, and fail to follow up and make adjustments to their investment combinations according to the stock market conditions. In reality, just as one's body requires regular checkups, we also need to regularly assess our investment portfolio. Is one of the stocks in the portfolio performing way below the average market level? Do you need to make any changes of fund managers for any of your funds? Also, remember to adjust your investment portfolio based on your investment period. For instance, when it is nearer to your retirement, the high-risk funds in your retirement investment portfolio should correspondingly decrease.

Index